Do**

Living Between Two Worlds ~~explores the ....~~
modern Witches trying to reconcile their spiritual path with
the demands of materialistic Western culture.

Is it appropriate, or even desirable to use the word
"Witch"? Should we all remain private or come out of the
"broom closet"? What do we do about requests for magic or
healing from non-Witches? Can a Witch also be a Christian? Eight modern Witches offer some answers to these
questions which have been the source of endless debate
within the Wiccan community.

"Between the worlds" has multiple meanings for a
Witch, and this book explores how to function effectively
within both the Otherworld of mystical experience and the
mundane world of everyday life.

Secrecy, sacred sexuality, ethics—each of the authors
included in this anthology addresses particular problems
and issues common to us all, sharing their personal experiences and offering sensible advice for the rest of us.

Insightful and informative, *Living Between Two Worlds*
reveals an aspect of this modern magical religion that often
gets forgotten—the practical facts of day-to-day life after the
festival and outside the magical circle.

About the Editor

Chas. S. Clifton holds a master's degree in religious studies with an emphasis on the development of new religious movements. He lives in the Wet Mountains of Colorado where he writes about Western esoteric traditions.

To Write to the Editor

If you wish to contact the editor or would like more information about this book, please write to the editor in care of Llewellyn Worldwide, and we will forward your request. Both the editor and publisher appreciate hearing from you. Llewellyn Worldwide cannot guarantee that every letter written to the editor can be answered, but all will be forwarded. Please write to:

Chas S. Clifton
c/o Llewellyn Worldwide
P.O. Box 64383, Dept. K151-1
St. Paul, MN 55164-0383, U.S.A.

Please enclose a self-addressed, stamped envelope for reply, or $1.00 to cover costs. If outside the U.S.A., enclose international postal reply coupon.

Free Catalog from Llewellyn

For more than ninety years Llewellyn has brought its readers knowledge in the fields of metaphysics and human potential. Learn about the newest books in spiritual guidance, natural healing, astrology, occult philosophy, and more. Enjoy book reviews, New Age articles, a calendar of events, plus current advertised products and services. To get your free copy of Llewellyn's New Worlds, send your name and address to:

Llewellyn's New Worlds of Mind and Spirit
P.O. Box 64383, Dept. K151-1
St. Paul, MN 55164-0383, U.S.A.

Llewellyn's Witchcraft Today Series
Book Four

Living

Between
Two Worlds

Challenges of the Modern Witch

Edited by Chas S. Clifton

1996
Llewellyn Publications
St. Paul, Minnesota 55164-0383

Photo illustration components: © 1995 Photo Disc, Inc. and Digital Stock Corporation

Cover design: Anne Marie Garrison
Editing and layout: Marguerite Krause
Project management and interior design: Amy Rost

FIRST EDITION
First Printing, 1996

Library of Congress Cataloging-in Publication Data

Living between two worlds : challenges of the modern
    witch / edited by Chas S. Clifton. -- 1st ed.
        p.   cm. -- (Witchcraft today : bk. 4)
    Includes bibliographical references (p.).
    ISBN 1-56718-151-1   (pbk.)
    1. Witchcraft. 2. Goddess religion. I. Clifton, Chas.
II. Series
BF1571.L58 1996   96-34112
133.4'3--dc20   CIP

Llewellyn Publications
A Division of Llewellyn Worldwide, Ltd.
P.O. Box 64383
St. Paul, Minnesota 55164-0383

For Mary

Previously Published Books in this Series

WITCHCRAFT TODAY, BOOK ONE:
The Modern Craft Movement

WITCHCRAFT TODAY, BOOK TWO:
Modern Rites of Passage

WITCHCRAFT TODAY, BOOK THREE:
Witchcraft & Shamanism

Editor's Note

Living Between Two Worlds is the fourth anthology in Llewellyn Publications' ongoing *Witchcraft Today* series. The series is named partly in honor of Gerald B. Gardner, who helped create the modern magickal religion of Wicca or Neopagan Witchcraft in the mid-twentieth century. His own book *Witchcraft Today,* published in 1954, was the first to present Wicca in its modern form instead of as a superstitious practice of "primitive" peoples or of bygone centuries.

The first anthology in this series, *The Modern Craft Movement,* discusses a wide range of topics from the sacramental use of sexuality to Wicca as an Earth religion to the legal and political problems faced by present-day Pagans. It was followed by *Modern Rites of Passage,* which is devoted to creating a living Pagan culture, exemplified by the basic stages of life: birth, puberty, partnership, and so forth.

The third volume, *Witchcraft & Shamanism,* examines historic shamanism and its links with Wicca, and discusses modern "neoshamanic" practices.

Throughout the *Witchcraft Today* series, I have capitalized Witchcraft and Witch when they refer to the modern magickal religion of Wicca and its followers. When not capitalized, the reference is to historical witchcraft (principally during the witch-trial period that lasted from the late Middle Ages into the eighteenth century) and to "witch" in the unfortunate anthropological sense of "evil magic-worker." Many contemporary Pagan writers also use the spelling "magick" to distinguish "The art of effecting changes in consciousness at will" from stage magic or other misconceptions created by outsiders.

—Chas S. Clifton

Table of Contents

Principles of Wiccan Belief

*In 1974, one group of American Witches meeting in Min-
neapolis adopted the following group of principles. Since
then, several versions of these principles, with minor differences in wording, have been circulated. These principles are not required of anyone, but they do reflect the
thinking of many modern Pagan Witches, whether in the
United States or elsewhere.*

The Council of American Witches finds it necessary to
define modern Witchcraft in terms of the American experience and needs.

We are not bound by traditions from other times and other
cultures, and owe no allegiance to any person or power
greater than the Divinity manifest through our own being.

As American Witches we welcome and respect all teachings and traditions, and seek to learn from all and to con-
tribute our learning to all who may seek it.

It is in this spirit of welcome and cooperation that we adopt these few principles of Wiccan belief. In seeking to be inclusive, we do not wish to open ourselves to the destruction of our group by those on self-serving power trips, or to philosophies and practices contradictory to those principles. In seeking to exclude those whose ways are contradictory to ours, we do not want to deny participation with us to any who are sincerely interested in our knowledge and beliefs.

We therefore ask only that those who seek to identify with us accept those few basic principles.

1. We practice rites to attune ourselves with the natural rhythm of life forces marked by the full of the Moon and seasonal quarters and cross-quarters.

2. We recognize that our intelligence gives us a unique responsibility toward our environment. We seek to live in harmony with Nature, in ecological balance offering fulfillment to life and consciousness within an evolutionary concept.

3. We acknowledge a depth of power far greater than that apparent to the average person. Because it is far greater than ordinary, it is sometimes called "supernatural," but we see it as lying within that which is naturally potential to all.

4. We conceive of the Creative Power in the Universe as manifesting through polarity—as masculine and feminine—and that this same Creative Power lives in all people, and functions through the masculine and feminine. We value neither above the other.

5. We value sex as pleasure, as the symbol and embodiment of life, and as the interaction source of energies used in magical practice and religious worship.

6. We recognize both an outer world and an inner, or psychological world—sometimes known as the Spiritual World, the Collective Unconscious, Inner Planes, etc.— and we see in the interaction of these two dimensions the basis for paranormal phenomena and magickal exercises. We neglect neither dimension for the other, seeing both as necessary for our fulfillment.

7. We do not recognize any authoritarian hierarchy, but do honor those who teach, respect those who share their greater knowledge and wisdom, and acknowledge those who courageously give of themselves in leadership.

8. We see religion, magic, and wisdom in living as being united in the way one views the world and lives within it—a worldview and philosophy of life that we identify as Witchcraft, the Wiccan Way.

9. Calling oneself "Witch" does not make a Witch—but neither does heredity itself nor the collecting of titles, degrees, and initiations. A Witch seeks to control the forces within her/himself that make life possible in order to live wisely and well, without harm to others and in harmony with Nature.

10. We believe in the affirmation and fulfillment of life in a continuation of evolution and development of consciousness giving meaning to the Universe we know and our personal role within it.

11. Our only animosity toward Christianity, or toward any other religion or philosophy of life, is to the extent that its institutions have claimed to be "the only way," and have sought to deny freedom to others and to suppress other ways of religious practice and belief.

12. As American Witches, we are not threatened by debates on the history of the Craft, the origins of various terms, the legitimacy of various aspects of different traditions. We are concerned with our present and our future.

13. We do not accept the concept of absolute evil, nor do we worship any entity known as "Satan" or "the Devil" as defined by the Christian tradition. We do not seek power through the suffering of others nor accept that personal benefit can be derived only by denial to another.

14. We believe that we should seek within Nature that which is contributory to our health and well-being.

Living Between Two Worlds

By Chas S. Clifton

For this is a time that is not a time
In a place that is not a place
On a day that is not a day

An invocation like this, expressing the "between the worlds" quality of the rituals of modern Witchcraft, describes how sacred space and time feel as though they are outside the boundaries of mundane time and space. "Between the worlds" has multiple meanings to the Witch or Pagan. There is, of course, its ritual or magical meaning: it straddles two realities, two modes of perception. Often these are called the Unseen World and the World of Form, the physical world. Magickal ritual requires its participants to realize that "everywhere is the center of the universe" and that they, at least for a set time, are conceptually freeing themselves from the limits of the everyday work with its clocks, calendars, and schedules.

Likewise, they are setting aside the material view that only the evidence of the physical senses and physically explainable forms of cause and effect are valid and rational. Witches see themselves at such times as having a foot both in the everyday world of the physical senses and in some more subtle realm, that space in which Time acts differently and where the currents and events of this world work themselves out before manifesting themselves to us.

When we lead ritual, we must move between altered or ecstatic states and some state permitting us to work with those in less-ecstatic states. No one spends all of his or her time in a ritual circle. We return to other worlds, to the quasi-tribal culture of Pagandom—and to the larger cultures, nations, and planet that we share. Here we experience different kinds of "betweenness."

One note: returning is important. As Lady Sheba, an influential American Wiccan teacher of the 1970s once said, too much time spent in inner-planes ecstasy can cause a person to become, as she put it, "astral enamored." This is why Ashleen O'Gaea's article, next in this book, is called "Griffins and Grocery Stores." The "and" is important. Witches look for the integration of magickal and mundane realities. We do not always succeed, but that is our goal— to go out and to come back. Some esoteric teachers have offered magic virtually as a form of cheap entertainment, less expensive than a ticket to the movie theater. The "not quite all here" sensation that Sheba identified is quite real. For the wrong person, it may lead to psychological problems. It is in a way irresponsible. In her book, *The Spiral Dance*, Starhawk writes, "When inner visions become a way of escaping contact with others, we are better off simply watching television."[1]

This feeling of being "between two worlds" also can occur when we attempt to reconcile magickal ways of thinking and what is loosely called a "scientific" world view. I put "scientific" in quotation marks because certain Witches, with a better grasp on the latest thinking in quantum physics than I have, suggest that that the two at some point may blend into each other. Meanwhile, we deal with metaphors such as "different truths" or "different planes."[2]

Cultural conflicts—or the potential for conflict—present another possible meaning for the phrase "living between two worlds." As members of what is still a minority religion, we take positions every day on how "public" we will be. As Valerie Voigt titled her chapter in the first volume of this series, *The Modern Craft Movement*, we are faced with "Being a Pagan in a 9-to-5 World"—and for the other hours of the day as well. To subscribe to a Pagan world view, of a divine force within all things without a separation of "creator" from "creation," of individual spiritual authority, is to set one's self against many cultural currents. The resulting conflicts have not only posed lively problems for Witches themselves; they have fueled debates within Pagandom that stretch on for decades—to use the word "Witch" or not, to be public or not, to actively promote the use of magical work or to sit back and await requests for help, to stand out from the crowd or to blend in.

Many Witches keep their religious identity a secret for purely practical reasons. Everyone in the Craft must take a stand on the issue of openness, or as the favorite cliché has it, "being in/out of the broom closet." We weigh our desire for self-expression and religious freedom against our perceived social power or lack of it. If we are legal minors, will we be penalized for going against family traditions? If we are university students, will we be marginalized for being "irrational"? If we are employees, will we find ourselves on the "slow track" in the workplace or out of a job all together? If we are parents, will we be judged "unfit" by some social-service agency or court? If we are married or in some other long-term relationship, will our spouses and lovers reject us as somehow tainted? If we are parents, will our own children see us as "weird"? If we assert religious rights publicly, will we be asked to jump through bureaucratic hoops that other traditions are permitted to ignore?

One Pagan, fresh from a victory over a prejudiced teacher at her daughter's school, will confidently announce, "As long as we cower in the broom closet, then we deserve to be persecuted. History is full of peoples who, because they were quiet or kept their beliefs to themselves or lived as a closed community, ended up being persecuted for it." Someone else will respond, "No one deserves to be persecuted. We should live openly but not force ourselves on other people. Just be ready to answer questions when they come up." Another voice will chime in with a cautionary tale about losing a job or having a run-in with Social Services because someone thought that "Pagan" or "Witch" meant "untrustworthy" or "bad parent."[3]

We have freely made our choices, most of us, in a culture that is generally willing to concede that religion is a "private matter." That general belief demonstrates a little benign hypocrisy—people's public actions often spring from religious beliefs—but it lets us live together. Nevertheless, in twenty years experience as a professed Pagan, I have seen many of the second type of "between the worlds" conflicts arise when we uphold values and accept a label that we feel sets us apart from a majority of the people around us at least some of the time.

Not only do many Wiccans wish to keep that part of their identity quiet, but some of our rituals are secret as well—not because they involve illegal activity but because many Witches believe that power talked-about is power dissipated. (Women-only and men-only rituals often end up being "secret" from the other sex as well.) I see a parallel in many writer friends who refuse to talk about work in progress, not for fear of having their ideas stolen, but because they fear that if they talk about it, they will never get around to writing it. Nevertheless, in a culture that appears to value "openness" and "equality," admitting that something is not completely open to anyone is to invite suspicion.

The secrecy issue has been around from the start of the twentieth-century Wiccan revival. During the early 1940s, the Craft began to take much of its present form in wartime England. Gerald Gardner, who contributed so much to that form, was active in the British Home Guard, a body of lightly armed civilians organized in the face of the German invasion planned for 1940.[4] It is, I believe, no coincidence that the Craft Laws ("Ordains" or "Ardanes") promulgated by his and parallel traditions lay out an apparatus for maintaining secrecy that owes much to the World War II Resistance movements of France, Norway, the Netherlands, and other occupied countries. While they were seemingly set in the sixteenth or seventeenth centuries, they were shaped by twentieth-century events.

After World War II came the Cold War. Events outside our control kept the Witchcraft/secrecy link alive. Now "witch hunt" became a common term for fanatical attempts to expose Communist agents believed active in government, education, the entertainment industry, or elsewhere. The American playwright Arthur Miller's drama *The Cauldron* drew upon the Salem "witch trials" of 1692 to show the effects of such suspicion, mistrust, and injustice.[5]

Between this historical legacy and the simple facts of modern life, is it any wonder that the issue of disclosure is an important one? Furthermore, as I will come to, there is more than one purpose for secrecy.

Thanks to efforts at public outreach and education reaching back to the mid-1950s in Britain and the mid-1960s in North America, the climate of opinion is slowly changing for the better. The numberless interviews granted (particularly in late October) and books written by the more public members of the Craft have had a real effect. Gavin Frost, a widely known Wiccan teacher and writer, recently told me that when he and his wife, Yvonne, traveled in the 1970s, they could get news media attention almost anywhere by simply saying "We're Witches." Now, he said, interest in Witchcraft merely for the sake of its exoticism has waned noticeably.

That is not to say that people always can ignore our presence long enough to hear what we have to say. For instance, when I appeared in September 1994 on a national radio talk show, several persons called in just to proclaim, "He should not be allowed on the air." Fortunately the host dealt with them smoothly and professionally.

This is, then, an era of distinctly mixed perception on the issue of just how public the Craft should be. Some

Wiccans will argue that being public is, in the long run, the best strategy. On the other hand Morven, the former editor of the Boston-based Pagan magazine *Harvest*, suggests in her article that at least some Witches can help the rest by staying "closeted" and working to improve Wicca's public image from within.

One recent survey showed that at least half of all Pagans were "moderately" secret while about a fifth were totally "in the broom closet."[6] As Judy Harrow points out in "'Tis Evil Luck to Speak of It: Secrecy and the Craft," "Every Witch or Pagan has the absolute right to decide for themselves who shall know how much about their religious affiliation." Real life, however, has a habit of tossing out hard questions, and Harrow goes on to treat some of the most ticklish that a Wiccan priest and priestess can face, such as determining what internal conflicts should ever be taken to outside authorities: the police, the courts, and so on.

Making the choice to follow a semi-secret mystery religion causes many Witches to feel doubly conscious of the differences between themselves and other people. At worst, this self-consciousness reduces the Craft to mere exhibitionism: "Look at us—we know something that you don't." Let us be frank: who at some time has not enjoyed the feeling of being in possession of a shared secret? However, this delicious knowledge wears thin after a while; no spiritual practice or popular religion can be built upon it.

Of course, no one writing for this volume advocates any sort of spiritual snobbery. In fact, when contributor Malcolm Brenner began "The Us-Them Dichotomy," he used an instance of misplaced religious snobbery to make a point about the distinct Craft world view, namely that we should not congratulate ourselves on being "chosen people." Magick requires a blend of self-confidence (often called "acting as if") and humility; smug Witches make poor magicians.

The issue of secrecy, in fact, may be larger than merely a question of disclosure or non-disclosure. For some Witches, a diminished role in the Pagan community may reflect a deliberate withdrawal in order to deepen their mystical and magickal practice.

Often, I have noticed, newcomers to Wicca move through a regular series of stages in their practice. First comes the seeker, full of longings, half-understood impulses, attempting to make contact with like-minded people who will teach him. This person, someone just setting out to follow the Old Religion, may discover valid psycho-magickal utility in the old rituals of separation. As recently as the early 1970s, a do-it-yourself Witchcraft book offered a phonetic guide to saying the Lord's Prayer backwards while visualizing "great iron shackles struck off your hands and feet by sizzling bolts of lightning and disintegrating into molten shards to either side of you."[7] The principle is valid, but the method might seem too offensively anti-Christian for many Witches today. Like so much else in a magickal path, it depends on the individual.

Then comes the new student or initiate, trying to learn everything at once, writing furiously in her Book of Shadows and, from time to time, getting a little dogmatic. Some will go from that stage into larger community roles: starting covens, publishing newsletters, organizing events and festivals, perhaps serving as a spokesperson for the Craft to the larger world. At her best, she projects a positive image for the Craft; at her worst, she merely becomes a politician embroiled in her local "witch wars."

Such a person, engaged in an expansive, outward-moving time in his or her religious life, might well argue that Witches who value society are marginalizing themselves, inviting some of the very ills that Judy Harrow identifies: alienation, paranoia, dysfunctional leadership, intellectual stagnation. However, Witches, ritual magicians, esotercists of any school (and perhaps also the monks and contemplatives of other traditions as well) face a different bind. We need be marginal some of the time in order to do what we need to do. As Morven points out in, "Why I Stay in the Broom Closet," a traditional magician's rule is, "Keep silent." The magickal worker needs a certain degree of insulation and psychic space in order to operate.

The Witch whose practice leads him or her into solitude for a time might be motivated by different things. One might be the demands of mundane life: a job, illness, family responsibilities. The motivation might also be a desire for retreat, for deepening. In my experience, the "political" phase of Wiccan work is often followed by an inward-turning retreat, an "inhalation," a search for a new position "between the worlds." Since the Craft has no monasteries, this "spiritual retreat" can only take place within the mundane life. Ritual magicians have designed (principally on paper) all kinds of "lodges," "chapter houses," "retreat houses," and the like. Some such institutions have even existed for a while. Likewise, some Wiccans have advocated communal living for both its economic and spiritual benefits. However, the "closeted" solitary Witch, or even the member of a non-public coven, can realize some of the benefits of a contemplative life. It may be expressed by wrapping into a cloak of secrecy, even as in other religions the renunciate's robe expresses that that person has separated himself or herself, to a large extent, from the demands of family or society.

This Witch would have moved beyond the superficial attractions of rebellion or nonconformity, of deliciously appreciating the special fact that she was "not like them." One of the century's best-known Christian monastic writers uses language here that could be adapted easily to a Wiccan context. When Thomas Merton wrote "solitary," he meant a contemplative monk or nun; he himself was a member of the Trappist or reformed Cistercian order. However, suppose that—without meaning any harm to his original text—we substitute the Wiccan meaning of the term "solitary": "The true solitary does not renounce anything that is basic and human about his relationship to other men—he renounces vain pretenses of solidarity that tend to substitute themselves for real solidarity, while masking an inner spirit of irresponsibility and selfishness."[8]

More stages might well follow, more movings-in and movings-out, inhalations and exhalations, dropping the cloak of secrecy to move in the outer world and then wrapping up in it again. In this sense, I suspect, the "closet" metaphor, while useful in an everyday sense, limits the range of possibilities in the Witch's life.

Them and Us, Us and Us

Outside observers, meanwhile, may wonder if Pagans do not see more of a rift between them and other people than there really is. One psychological anthropologist who observed Wiccans and ritual magicians in Britain noted,

Whether or not magical ideas are incompatible with, say, the teachings of a university faculty of physics is not at issue. What is important is the perception that they are not. Magicians seemed to feel that the larger society around them assumed the incompatibility.[9]

Sociologists have ascribed this feeling of separation partly to "status inconsistencies." According to one set of researchers, modern Pagans are likely to be relatively highly educated in relation to their incomes. Thus, he concludes, "Pagan Witches are under-rewarded status discontents who care little for money and much for knowledge."[10]

On the other hand, it may be that modern Pagans over-emphasize their differentness, their "marginality," for their own purposes. Part of the question involves the fluid definitions of the word "witch." Is it true, as the same sociologists concluded, that "Most [Wiccan 'insiders'] definitions of Witchcraft are organizational rather than mystical or psychic"?[11] If it is, then maybe someone merely wants the pay-off without the work. The public, however, while more likely than a generation ago to accept the definition of Wicca-as-religion that so many modern Witches have struggled to promulgate, still also accepts the older definition of a "witch" being a person with certain somewhat ambiguous magical powers. At times, out of need or curiosity, they ask for magickal help.

When these requests arrive, too many Wiccans are paralyzed. Their typical first response is to suggest a reading list, which is about the last thing that the inquirer usually wants. Perhaps we are confusing the issues of helping someone with an immediate problem with offering them an open door into the Craft. Not everyone wants to be a

Witch. Imagine, for instance, if someone approached a Roman Catholic priest in the same vein:

Seeker: "I have such-and-such a problem, Father. Will you pray for me?"

Catholic priest: "Only if you read these books first."

Granted, if the seeker were seeking admission into the Catholic Church, then religious instruction appropriate to the person would be required. Frankly, having seen Neo-pagan Witches execute all sorts of evasive maneuvers when asked for magickal assistance by an outsider, I am inclined to think that much of some Pagans' resistance to the word "Witch" lies not in the fact that that it merely has unpleasant connotations but rather that its use can create a severe case of performance anxiety. Say that you are a "Witch" and people will ask your help. It's as simple as that—and as challenging.

As Paul Suliin writes in his article, "Cast Me a Spell: The Witch as Magical Technician," "Magical work may be the only contact some non-Pagans ever have with the Craft." That being the case, and extending the term "magical work" to include acts such as Tarot readings or marriage celebrations, he offers guidelines and examples of effective and ethical ways to respond to that request for magick-working.

Neither Paul Suliin nor I would suggest that the deepest purpose of the Craft is to build up "powers" and an ego to go with them. On the other hand, if modern Witches see ourselves as specialists, technicians, practitioners, then we should take the responsibility to helping those people who overcome their fear—or skepticism—to seek us out. We say that we are all more clergy than congregation; well, then, let's be aware of the responsibilities that go with the task.

Revived Witchcraft arose in literate cultures of the twentieth-century; therefore, modern Witches have always seen themselves reflected in the news media, in books, films, and television productions, and also in academic writing. At first, scholarly examination of the Craft concentrated on upholding or attacking its historical claims, the rapidly eroding notion of an unbroken, self-aware chain of belief and practice stretching back to pre-Christian Europe.[12] More recently—since the 1980s mainly—we have looked into the mirrors held up by sociologists and anthropologists who began to ask their own questions about who the modern Witches were. Some attempted to jam us into the categories created by the systems' founders, scholars such as Max Weber and Emile Durkheim, who saw the certainties of nineteenth-century Christianity shaken by the Industrial Revolution.[13] Drawing on these older categories, they proclaimed that "Pagans lessen their felt powerlessness through the practice of magic; lessen their isolation with the coven; and lessen their anomie with the folkloric 'traditions.'"[14]

Others have attempted the morally ambiguous task of becoming "participant-observers," seeking initiation into covens while inwardly remaining outsiders and observers. "I am one of the few anthropologists who could not be [visually] distinguished from their field," proudly claimed one researcher into Wicca and ceremonial magic, confronting the stereotype of the pith-helmeted anthropologist among the "natives."[15]

This participant-observer approach, in my experience, almost always leads to hurt feelings, even when the researcher is open about it from the first. Someone is going to be lied to somewhere along the line. It may be the group under observation, the researcher's academic colleagues, or the reading public. In some cases, the "participant-observer" stance may lead to acts of disrespect such as one I witnessed when a graduate student in anthropology attempted to perform a Wiccan ritual in front of an under-graduate anthropology class—one "outsider" explaining us to other "outsiders." (I was present as a journalist, definitely "between worlds" on that day!)

Certain that they could do a better job if given the chance, by the mid-1980s a number of Witches began to pursue graduate degrees in such fields as anthropology, sociology, religious studies, and psychology. Others, indeed, had already done so, but the newcomers were more open about, first, their own religion and, second, their desire to devote at least some of their academic attentions to it.

To follow the Pagan path today, whether in the broadest philosophical sense or within the more focused, initiatory sense (or a combination of the two) is a conscious choice, a choice that makes these issues of openness so keen. There are relatively few "cradle Pagans" among us, but someday there will be more.[16] Our own teachings demand that we offer our children the same choice that we claimed for our-selves, even while we might hope that they will continue upon what we have built.

Other Issues of "Between-ness"

Another perception that others may have of the Craft, a per-ception that has been fostered by years of sensationalism (centuries, if one chooses examples from the Burning Times), is that we are sexually busier than everyone else. This image got a boost during the so-called "sexual revolution" of the

1960s and early 1970s. For example, one mass-market paperback book from that era, titled *The Naked Witch*, proclaimed on its cover, "A real, wildly wicked witch shares her secrets for greater sexual power and pleasure."[17]

In fact, as Rhiannon Asher writes in her article, "When Sex is a Sacrament," there is a unique Wiccan attitude towards sex—but it does not depend on the cliché of the "sexual swinger." Understanding sexuality's sacred dimension is the real sexual revolution. The "secret" missing from approaches like *The Naked Witch's* involves the Witch's understanding that sex can involve both raw physical desires and worship of the divine simultaneously.

In the end, no matter how we draw boundaries, someone will come along who defies them. The Pagan community has long been troubled by those "leaders" who would decide who was "in" and who was "out"—the action not of a spiritual exemplar but of a religious politician. Religious politicians, however—whatever their affiliation—might be surprised at the Reverend B., author of "Priestess and Pastor: Serving Between Two Worlds." Not only is she a priestess and Witch, leading a coven in a Western city, but she is also an ordained minister in a mainline Protestant denomination although not currently holding a pastoral appointment, having switched to university teaching. Her statement, "I am both Pagan priestess and Christian pastor. I serve between the worlds," might shock nearly as many Pagans—proportionately—as it does Christians. Here is one of "them" saying that she is also one of "us!" Our stated Pagan tolerance for diversity in religion, for refusing to certify absolute doctrinal "truth," would ring false if we did not accept the possibility that she offers. The shock her position has created among some Pagans merely indicates that they are still prisoners of monotheistic categories. If Jesus is among the Dying Gods, then, this contributor could well offer, she can invoke him as well and as truly as anyone else could.

I began with lines from a typical ritual invocation that spoke the language of "living between the worlds." Lest we become too involved in the mundane uses of the phrase, Ashleen O'Gaea brings us back to the importance of the Otherworld in Craft practice. We must shift realities and function effectively in each. "When we give these experiences to ourselves and each other—literally or symbolically—we are drawing down the Otherworld and grounding ourselves in Wholeness, the matrix of our individual lives," she says. "This is part of our nature and part of our natural range. To survey our everydays from the wider perspective we get between the worlds is both challenging and sublimely useful. And that is the reason, of course, for taking the trouble to live between the worlds."

Notes

1. Starhawk, *The Spiral Dance* (San Francisco: Harper & Row, 1979), 192.

2. For one psychological anthropologist's attempt to define magicians' and Witches' different cognitive coping strategies, see chapter nine of T.M. Luhrmann, *Persuasions of the Witch's Craft: Ritual Magic in Contemporary England* (Cambridge, Massachusetts: Harvard University Press, 1989). Luhrman speaks of the "realist," "two-worlds," "relativist," and "metaphorical" positions towards the apparent differences between the magickal and scientific world views.

3. Instances of Pagans being reported to departments of social services merely for their religious beliefs have multiplied in recent years, although the earliest involving someone whom I personally knew took place in the 1970s and resulted in the woman involved losing custody of her two sons. Another friend was more lucky—the social worker was an American Buddhist and knew how members of minority religions are sometimes treated.

4. The magickal workings of that summer by the British Witches against Hitler's invasion plan have not only become a cornerstone legend of the Craft, they gave the British Craft—at least to itself—a set of patriotic credentials unequaled elsewhere, as well as a metaphoric stance *vis-a-vis* Christianity.

5. Although the "Salem witch" image lives on, I do not believe that the events three hundred years ago had anything to do with Pagan religion. The so-called witches went to their deaths protesting that they were good Christians.

6. Stewart Farrar, Janet Farrar and Gavin Bone, *The Pagan Path* (Custer, Washington: Phoenix Publishing, 1995), 221.

7. Paul Huson, *Mastering Witchcraft* (New York: G.P. Putnam's Sons, 1970), 23.

8. Thomas Merton, *Disputed Questions* (New York: New American Library, 1965 [1960]), 145.

9. Luhrmann, 12.

10. R. George Kirkpatrick, Rich Raney, and Kathryn Rubi, "Pagan Renaissance and Wiccan Witchcraft in Industrial Society: A Study in Parasociology and the Sociology of Enchantment." *Iron Mountain: A Journal of Magical Religion 1* (Summer 1984), 38.

11. Ibid, 35.

12. One of the first attacks on the doctrine of "unbroken Craft tradition stretching back to pre-Christian Europe" came in Eliot Rose's *A Razor for a Goat* (Toronto: University of Toronto Press, 1962).

13. Max Weber (1864–1920), a German founder of sociology, wrote extensively on religion, most notably on how the attitudes and teachings of Protestant Christianity aided the rise of large-scale capitalism. Emile Durkheim (1859–1917), who taught in Bordeaux and Paris, also studied religion's role in integrating the individual into social life.

14. Kirkpatrick et al., 37.

15. Luhrmann, 17. She also notes (p. 10) that her American accent instantly placed her outside the British preoccupation with social class.

16. Some "cradle Pagans," however, were interviewed by California writer Anodea Judith for her chapter on Pagan adolescence in *Witchcraft Today Book 2: Modern Rites of Passage.*

17. Gay-Darlene Bidart, *The Naked Witch* (New York: Pinnacle Books, 1975). It includes penis-reading as a (tongue-in-cheek?) form of divination.

About the Author

Chas S. Clifton lives in the southern Colorado foothills, where in recent years he has worked as a newspaper reporter, counted owls in nearby mountains for the Bureau of Land Management, and taught university writing classes. In addition to editing Llewellyn's *Witchcraft Today* series, he is the author of *The Encyclopedia of Heresies and Heretics* (ABC-Clio, 1992). He is a contributing editor for *Gnosis,* and his column, "Letters from Hardscrabble Creek," is carried in several Pagan magazines.

Griffins and Grocery Stores:
Everyday Life Between the Worlds

By Ashleen O'Gaea

To talk about living between the worlds, we have to have some idea of what worlds we might be living between. The conventional understanding is that another world/Other-world exists simultaneously with the physical environment we're aware of—in Earth's aura or in an adjacent dimension or in our brains' synapses, merely concealed from our limited human sight by some meta-mystical means. We know that the Otherworld is vast and contains as many regions as there have ever been cultures. Like the physical universe, the Otherworld is expanding to embrace yet more visions as life evolves. In some places its borders are sharply drawn and abruptly crossed, as through a mist or down a hole or hollow trunk; sometimes the boundaries are imperceptible, and you know that you have crossed them only upon your first Encounter. Some bits of the Otherworld are bounded by a sort of easement where folks from both worlds can meet on neutral or common ground, *between* the worlds—

reminiscent of the way Druid priests traveled at will through warring territories. The idea of an Otherplace with Other rules and Other ways of measuring people's worth is so much a part of our perceptual psychology that it is reflected in the way we see our everyday lives.

For instance, we have our "regular" lives: the grocery store, job, laundry, in-laws, school, taxes, construction detours. Then we have our "real" lives, doing what we love: gardening, camping, cooking, art, ritual, singing, parenting, skydiving, personal things. Those two parts of our lives are like two worlds. For covening Witches, "living between two worlds" is, among other things, an effort to reconcile and/or find time and energy to meet the demands of priestess and employer. Living between the worlds challenges us more meaningfully, invites and requires us to reach deeper into ourselves, and rewards us more faithfully than the artificial lives too many of us call "everyday."

"Between the worlds" betokens much in the Pagan community and, because it is metaphoric, it means many things, often simultaneously. Liturgically, the phrase has a traditional meaning: the ritual circle is "a boundary between the world of men and the realms of the Mighty Ones," as Janet and Stewart Farrar put it,[1] and when it is cast, "we are between the Worlds."[2] However, experience is wider than liturgy, and so, in our lives and through the years, "between the worlds" describes adventures in many venues.

Between the worlds, familiar landmarks and our vision of them are transformed. We leave behind the grocery stores and anticipate griffins—the ordinary follows us not. Though the everyday walls of home are standing where they were left, Witches admitted to the circle are somewhere else. Unconstrained by his lordship's agenda or the boss's, unmolested by social expectations and economic concerns, a Witch walks between the worlds, an equal to life, empowered and belovèd. It is this experience the circle promises to those who cast it to adore Her—She Who is queen of all the Witches.[3] This is the reality that still inspires Witches to take the risks they must to cast Moon and sabbat circles.

The reality is that we *need* the Otherworld and the halls and anterooms between the worlds, the same as we need food, sleep, each other, clean air, all the forests. We need these interfaces in our lives, halls long enough for the trains of ladies' gowns, forests mysterious enough for the most precious herbs, companionship trusty enough to carry us through the bleakest chases. When we give these experiences to ourselves and each other—literally or symbolically—we are drawing down the Otherworld and grounding ourselves in Wholeness, the matrix of our individual lives. This is part of our nature and part of our natural range. To survey our everydays from the wider perspective we get between the worlds is both challenging and sublimely useful. That is the reason, of course, for taking the trouble to live between the worlds. The adventure, the wonder, calls us; we long for the richness of mystery we associate with the Otherworld. Some religions forbid us to step between the worlds, but with perfect love of what we know of the world and ourselves, and perfect trust of what we've not yet discovered, Witchcraft encourages us to cross the threshold. Holding less fast to routine (and holding our routines and presumptions accountable), cultivating an interest in new perspectives, exploring unfamiliar precepts, taking responsibility for our attitudes, and seeing our selves and our lives in new ways, helps us blend, each of us uniquely, "the best of both worlds."

The best includes the individual spiritual benefits of self-discovery, one of the evolutionary benefits that have kept the calling alive in our genes with its diversity intact. Living between the worlds, always called to see what lies around the next bend, ready to see the instant challenge as an adventure, restores the depths of wonder and the thrill of anticipation to our experiences with the promise of many-layered meaning and affirmative interpretation. Living between the worlds, we're aware of the interconnections among us, we can see the strands of the Web, so to speak, and experience the one-ness.

"The advent of a highly sophisticated scientific community that consequently produced a runaway technology has caused an ever-widening gulf between 'daily life' and 'spirituality' among discerning educated people, particularly in Europe and the United States. This chasm is more than separation of church from state; it is separation of 'Self' from 'Spirit' or animating Life Force," says Carol Lee Sanchez in an article about new world tribal communities.[4] She also believes it is important to "make sacred, to acknowledge the new ways and elements in our lives—from nuclear power …to plastics and computers. It is time now, again, for the entire world to honor…these new molecular forms in order to restore harmony and balance."[5] Whether these "new molecular forms" come from labs or reveal themselves through experience, it is important to "honor these Spirits," as Sanchez puts it. It is the (purposeful) consideration of all our experiences and environments as alive and true, real and valuable, that puts us "between the worlds."

Trained by all kinds of cultural experience, we have a mostly unrecognized expectation that things are going to happen quickly. "Plastics and computers," reducing a week's calculation to a moment's, have atrophied our patience. A six-month investment is called long-term. On television, problems are resolved in an hour or less—in the movies, three hours at most. Our lives are compartmentalized, because if we felt the natural connections among ourselves we wouldn't support—we wouldn't permit!—the thousands of exploitations that have become so profitable on this planet. In the Craft, this socio-cultural background shows up in our expectation that there is a spell for everything, and it will all be taken care of by the next full Moon.

Not true. We take nine months to develop in the womb, not a sign that magic should be expected to work "overnight." Wondering what magic makes us live between the worlds, I answer that we are looking at lengthy spells, work that can take *years*. It is true that when we cast our circles or when we make ready for a camping trip, we cue ourselves and thus facilitate the impending change of consciousness. Just as in live theater, though, the prompter— the robes and ritual poses or the late-night packing of tents in cars—cannot carry you through the performance or between the worlds. Our rituals but mark the gates; it is up to each of us to step across the threshold, to do the inner work. To live between the worlds, the spell we must cast is for minds open to fearless reception of new information and unfamiliar points of view. We must learn to appreciate the whole of our experience (even the thoughts and feelings that we have been taught are unworthy) as possible, and to realize our own strength and obligations. The ritual we must enact requires us to *change* our mundane lives in response to the progress, over the years, of our inner work.

"Between the worlds" is a state of being, a state of doing, a state of seeing, that is slightly different for each of us; we speak of it conceptually, so that it becomes a way of talking about experience that is impossible to articulate otherwise. Between the worlds, we feel a one-ness with everything; when we are between the worlds, "everything" is a far wider category than usual. We talk about that in mythical terms because we recognize in the old stories the same effort we make to integrate the all-encompassing perspective (Wholeness) with the mundane, earth-bound point of view (Individuality). We're looking to bring some practical or at least familiar understanding to the Otherworld, and some of the Otherworld's magic to this.

To do this *à la carte* is possible, logistically. You can look at each circumstance of your life separately and "decorate" it with lovely magical effects, and if there is not much going on, that might work. However, the piecemeal approach does not make it any easier, by disconnecting your life, to keep the Rede,[6] and it takes a lot of energy to boot. It goes a little slower to take a holistic approach to living between the worlds, but it lays a stronger groundwork. As most Witches know and affirm, the preparation for magic is as important as the rite or spell itself. For us, preparation for the magic of living between the worlds is as much left-brained as right; we point out often that "it takes a lot of planning to be spontaneous."[7] So when I talk about living between the worlds, I am talking about and *advocating* taking the long way, the steep and rocky path, because in my experience, that's the route that properly prepares us to appreciate our destinations. Our group, Campsight, does not offer any shortcuts, but we offer the chalice and warm harmony around the campfire to other travelers in the wood.

Because our experience of other worlds is so romanticized in the popular culture—our imagery is primarily medieval and Western European—we must take special care not to mistake our symbols for literal reality, not to anthropomorphize our expectations or bias our receptivity. Sure, like the hapless, heroic characters of myth and fairy-tale, you might be wandering along most innocently, suddenly to find yourself habiting the Otherworld, conversing with its people, doing its deeds. It's great when that happens, but life between the worlds is often less dramatic. If it were all to do with griffins and golden castles, we would notice it more often. More often, however, it has to do with the integration of individuality and wholeness within each of us.

When we cast a circle, we put our personal lives and our duty lives together in "the pleasant world of men" and call anything beyond that "the dread domains of the Lords of the Outer Spaces."[8] When we tell stories to our children, we put our personal and duty lives together in the ordinary world, and look for Arthur and Robin and Peter in the Otherworld, with all the archetypical creatures of myth and hope, in an approximately Jungian atmosphere of collective unconscious. (C. G. Jung's "and" approach, in contrast to other psyche-constructs' "or" perspectives, make his framework popular with Pagans of many traditions.) Exploring James Hillman's extended grasp of Jung, Daniel C. Noel offers some useful advice when he writes that "The...strategy now is to realize that nothing, not even literal fact, is absolutely real."[9] If there is no Platonic absolute standard of reality, then no one world has an exclusive claim to authority. All the worlds are, potentially, equally valid, and all of them equally necessary. The point is that wherever we are, whatever we can see, however we think about life, there is *more,* there is *different,* there is *other.* Just as life on the planet is widely and delightfully varied, with success not limited to one species per environment, so are there many successful "other" approaches we can take to our own lives. Not only is it *all right* to look at our lives from more than one point of view, but being stuck in one perspective can be pathological!

Modern Craft traditions are excitingly diverse, which strengthens us with the reminder that more than one safe path winds through the woods of life. Because we each experience the God/dess in our own way, we each describe reality in our own terms and interpret "between the worlds" in terms of our particular life's idioms. Yet for most of us, in whatever details, the concept affirms a depth and breadth beyond the ordinary,[10] and for most of us, it's a positive affirmation. For my family and coven, as for many, living between the worlds both requires and is defined by a confident assumption of *power with.* It means that the trees and rocks and beasts of the wood matter too, and it means that we're all in this together. We being the *de facto* wardens of the planet are responsible for weighing the rest of life's needs on the same scales as our own and honoring those needs in the decisions we make.

In the sense that each of us has to cope with several different sets of expectations and etiquettes in our lives, nobody lives in one world all the time, and many worlds in which we live influence our self-actualization. Living between the worlds is a capacity, a talent and a process, a function of our self-awareness—"individuation," Jung called it. As we are forced on/by the physical plane to be more sensitive to our "inter-eco-connections," re/cognizing other worlds becomes a more acceptable social behavior. More and more people are recalling that a natural world coexists with the asphalt jungle, remembering that we have roots in the natural world, and realizing that we need to protect those roots—and stems and leaves and berries.

"By root and stem, by leaf and bud" in one version or another is a common enough invocation among Witches, because we have known since ancient times that we are all rooted in and stem from one another. In a Wiccan circle, cast between the worlds, we rely upon ritual that, if not *truly* ancient, feels ancient, and thus reconnects us with ancestral attitudes of relatedness to life, the universe, and everything. In circle, and in all the rites and magic we undertake within it, we feel our power in the context of the Wholeness, and we find that as we become "one with everything," we are expanded, not annihilated. At camp, our tents pitched between the worlds, it is obvious to us that we are part of everything—hummingbirds mistake us for giant flowers almost every trip! Our power is like one voice in a mighty harmonic chorus, which as often as possible we manifest around the evening campfire. (We spend as much time as we can at camp, and usually our days and nights are filled with ritual and magic. We enjoy "high hokey pokey"[11] in the Woo-ids,[12] but I must confess that our favorite camping trips are between the Sabbats, when we can delight in the magic of life, the woods and everything, just appreciate that it's there and pursuing its own nature whether we are a-conjuring or no.) "Power over" is of little use in the woods; only "power with" will keep us warm and dry and safe for the night.

Once at the Citadel, a Sinaguan ruin at the Wupatki National Monument, I found a quetzal[13] feather—a blue and gold macaw feather, according to a covener who knows tropical birds (which do not live in northern Arizona). However, you do not have to come across a quetzal or glimpse a griffin, either, to be enriched by its flight. It's not *really* an either-or world, and we do not naturally see the world in the "zero-sum"[14] terms so familiar to us now. We do naturally make distinctions between ourselves and others, yes—as kin whose differences bring honor and power to our houses as various knights' adventures brought honor and power to Arthur's court. You do not doubt these companions when they are out of your sight! The kinship is of perfect love and perfect trust, such that whatever dangers threaten from without, in camp with your companions (wherever that is for you) you're safe.

Psychologist Jean Shinoda Bolen says that "a safe place psychologically is within a relationship . . . in which you can be in touch with your thoughts, feelings and sensations without being punished, judged or abandoned for having them. It is a place where you can trust that you will not be lied to and will be free of exploitation, where the other does not feel superior at your expense, does not betray your confidences or intrude upon your boundaries."[15] This is the relationship humans had with the Gods and the worlds for a long time, and one we can restore even now. Between the worlds we stand in perfect love and perfect trust, inviolate, in communion with truth and unbetrayed. It is to this "place" we go when we circle between the worlds, and for this "place" we long all our other hours; it is the atmosphere of this "place" we seek to recreate in the details of our lives and relationships.

There must be space in our lives to affirm and act out those values and expectations, space apart from our commercial and social electronic temples; that space is between the worlds. We must keep a place in this world for the Other, and that "place" is in our hearts, in our attitudes, in our relationship with the planet and all Her realms and systems. We must not feel superior at each other's expense, nor at the mountain gorillas' or the redwoods' or the elves' expense. We must not betray our brothers and sisters in the Craft nor our five-and-a-half billion brothers and sisters in humanity and our uncounted relations in the other "kingdoms." We must not intrude upon each other's boundaries, nor stress our skies and fields beyond their tolerances. Living between the worlds is living in that awareness—"living lightly," some call it—respecting and accommodating equally not only the concerns and demands of "both" worlds, but also each one's resources and opportunities.

Today, the promise of the circle, cast outdoors and in, still outweighs the risks (though the "stakes" are still high). Keeping the faith that keeps us, we still undertake our quests, we still make our pilgrimages between the worlds. Yours may take you to a favorite meadow or hill, to a trusted priestess's garage, or around your own living room thrice to the center. Ours take us to southeastern Arizona's national forests, and when we are city-bound, into yards and parks. We call our style of Witchcraft "Adventure" because we take our cue from our ancestors, historical and cultural, formal and informal, whose courage and zeal in exploring the worlds was unparalleled. Their approach to that exploration has taught us loyal camaraderie, curiosity, confidence and to celebrate of our differences. In many of

Adventure's sources, magic is a matter-of-fact part of every-day life. A pattern of bird-flight or a nut roasting on the fire makes an omen, and we read these as well as traffic signs on our ways around. Our understanding of magic is that *acting as if* makes it so. This is why ancient priests acted out pro-ductive hunts, and why in our spells Witches visualize our goals as already achieved; doing so changes our perception of reality, consistent with Doreen Valiente's suggestion that magic is "the art of changing consciousness at will." Thus, if we want to move between the worlds, we must *act as if* we can and do.

We can *act as if* in many ways, including the ways we cast and conduct our circles, when, in robes or shadow, our hair down, the chalice gleaming in the candlelight, it is easy to forget the corner market and the stock market. In the woods, it is obvious to us that these pawprints in the streambank could as easily be a baby griffin's as a skunk's. How to *act as if* at the altar of the paycheck can be a tougher question. Imagine striding down narrow castle corridors (is sunlight dappling those walls?) or through towering pines (conjure the scent) and spreading oaks, instead of just through the office or across the street from the bus stop. Compose ballads about people who catch your attention. Dedicate your work on a tedious project to the Goddess and see if She does not help you lighten it a bit. Maybe you cannot forget that you are a "working stiff," but you must also remember who else you are. One way to remember is quite consciously to decide that whatever place you are in, you will remember that it is not the only place you belong. In the tradition of Adventure (among others) the aim is not to integrate the worlds but to achieve a personal integra-tion that lets us live with an equal sense of recognition, belonging, comfort, and facility in "this world and all the worlds, in this time and all times."[16] If there is no place in our inner landscape for another world, then we'll never wander into it no matter how resoundingly is cast the circle, no matter how deep the forest where we camp.

In guided meditations we might rest our left brains between the worlds in some pleasant glen, but living between the worlds, like circling and camping, engages our logic as well as our intuition. In the circle and in the woods, the *more in heaven and earth* than Horatio dreamt of in his philosophy is "in your face." In the one case we conjure and call it forth, and in the other it conjures and calls us forth! In both cases, the Otherworld is impressed upon more senses and centers than our mundane training can override. Yet most of our time is spent in the mundane world, where secrecy (or at least subtlety) must still shield us from other people's ignorance and fear, and where we are constrained by standards and deadlines that might not make much sense to us "really." Further, to the extent that reintegrating ourselves by living between the worlds can be called healing, we are sometimes frustrated to find that our ordinary world isn't "really" structured to support that sort of health! (You can "spin" this power, too, of course; this "dystructure" offers a wealth of opportunity to share the healing we experience between the worlds. Indeed, many modern Witches do just that, focusing our magic on regeneration and growth.)

The trick to living between the worlds is knowing when to fall back on which standardized description of reality (Emily Post's? Gerald Gardner's?) and when to follow our gut and take another view of things. Twentieth-century scientists had to take a new look at things when

Isaac Newton's description of reality didn't work in the "dread domains…of the Outer Spaces"[17] where no science had gone before. They had to follow their instincts and invent new physics! Only by daring such new perspectives could they (and we) explore and hope to understand the worlds beyond Newton's sphere. Witches too learn to change their perspectives at will, from "participant" to "observer," finding each point of view tempered by the other. Folk wisdom has understood this for years: other perspectives don't have to be threatening. They are more often magical (or at least useful). That's why the Old Couple's children were always Setting Off Into the World to Find their Fortune—those were not just economic jaunts. Those youngest sons and daughters—who usually had their parents' blessings—were out to meet their *destinies,* to discover by adventure their own unique Individual relationship to the Whole; there was more to success than bags of coin and treasure and, often as not, an adventurer's fortune was won by fresh perspective. These images have long illuminated folk tales the world over, and link all our cultures to an ancient, common ancestral memory, the golden age of at-one-ment, the "dreamtime," that grounds most religions.

Talking about humanity's dreamtime,[18] Jean Shinoda Bolen says in *Ring of Power,*[19] "It is a time when humans are part of nature and can tap into the wisdom of the earth. Like the [world ash] tree whose branches reach high into the sky and whose roots reach down into the earth, the mental and physical realms come together; the underworld and the upper world are of equal importance." Finding more dreamtime in our mundane lives is a challenge, though; you can't very well ride to town on a griffin, and you can't camp every weekend. In practical terms, "living between the worlds" comes down to balancing the mundane and the mythic in our lives generally, deliberately as well as intuitively.

One way we can keep our lives between the worlds is to bring that wide perspective to the narrowest straits of our lives. That difficult co-worker wasn't born to plague you; s/he's working out compelling issues. You can choose to recognize the importance of that person's struggle and take the honorable roll of comprehending witness. The crop failure that drove grocery store prices sky high? "Amortize" that across the globe and across our ten thousand years of agricultural life, and let a sense of shared experience recompense you. Remember, you are not trying to *substitute* some swashbuckling fantasy for the practical reality of your ordinary life, you are trying to remember that no matter how outrageous or desanctified modern forms may be, underneath it all there is still a meaning to life. The meaning, the core, the mystery with which we reconnect between the worlds, is Wholeness and our condition of relationship with it. Wholeness is inclusive. Individuality, our present mode, has to be exclusive to some degree, else we wouldn't be able to tell ourselves apart in a mirror! Between the worlds we can experience the Wholeness and our Individuality simultaneously. Between the worlds there is room for the ordinary bits of our lives, even if our ordinary lives crowd and ignore the Otherworld. (It can be a life's initiatory task to understand and evaluate the world views presented to us by the mainstream and in our familiar circles and reinterpret them—or create new ones—in the mytho-cultural forms that mean the most to us.) We can learn to "translate" our mundane trials and tribulations into sacred terms—Challenge, Sacrifice, Initiation—and direct the energy they raise

away from our ulcer and anger zones! It's not uncommon
for adventurers to face a variety of trials before winning
through to the object of the quest, after all. (This is not an
attitude to take in lieu of filing appropriate harassment or
other discrimination charges, though.)

It helps to mythologize other people's boorish behavior;
don't take it personally. It's about them and the role(s) they
have assumed, about their perspectives. You are neither to
blame nor responsible. How you use your own resources in
response is what counts, what matters is what magic you
make with the energy mundane circumstances raise. At
their most basic, the discouraging agents and events of our
lives are nothing more than unmucked cow barns; if you
step in some of the muck on your way through, you just
have to find a garden where you can turn it into fertilizer.
(This is just one of a Witch's magic powers .)

Between the worlds our experience is that things are
not, and need not always be, what they seem or profess
themselves to be. There are deeper natures and meanings
that we can not only discover, but shape. One of the ways
we can change the shape of things is to change the way we
look at them. Things look different from the top of the hill
than they do from the floor of the valley. At least sometimes, it is important to take the wider perspective, to show
yourself that the bit of the world that dominates your life is
not all there is — it isn't even the only significant bit. Climb
the hill sometimes, literally and figuratively, and see that
your house is just one in the village, your village is just one
in the valley, your valley is just one of many among the
mountains, and your mountains are but one of the features
of this planet. Choose to see that the bit of any world you
need to change is not such a big bit after all[20] and allow

your confidence to be refreshed by new perspectives; perspective is relationship with God/dess. It has been, since the time before time, a Witch's way to wander between the worlds at will. Whether we call it a landscape or a mind-scape, the Otherworld touches us, and we touch it; there is no one who is not living between the worlds! The only question is whether we live in *awareness* of that fact.

Swept along by the current of the mainstream, unable to "go camping" every weekend, we have to deliberately learn the art and practice the skill of changing our percep-tions and being aware of changing the worlds—even with the copier's or the dishwasher's hum instead of humming-birds in the background. The moonlit dance in the field, the songful libation to the apple tree, the charm under the pillow—these were, are, and evermore shall be precious aspects of Witches' lives. Our coven has found it worth our while to go out of our way to give those ancestral images substance in our lives. Many of us were and still are told that these are the sorts of "things of childhood" we're sup-posed to put away when we grow up; these elements of our pagan culture are features of a devalued environment. This makes it both difficult and imperative to re/claim some of our lives' vigor for love and trust, to raise the energy, to clap our hands and bring Tinkerbell back to life, if you will. We must take the DANGER signs off our mem-ories and dreams, learn to know and nurture our strengths and eccentricities, dare to lie naked on a grassy slope in sheer celebration of being alive. When we do that, literally or symbolically, we have stepped between the worlds. Every time we do, our perception is altered just a little bit more. Perception's influence on reality varies in sort and degree from circumstance to "chronostance," but it is *always* present. This is, of course, the foundation of magic: changing our perceptions changes the worlds. Between the worlds, in awareness, meditation and exploration of other attitudes to take toward life and other presumptions than the ones we might take for granted, you change—every day—this world, your life in this world, and the relationship between the worlds.[21]

Notes

1. Stewart and Janet Farrar, *A Witches Bible Compleat, Vol. One* (New York: Magickal Childe, 1984), 38.

2. A conventional proclamation when the circle is fully cast.

3. This is a phrase from the Charge of the Goddess, common in one version or another to most Craft traditions. In Campsight's *Book of Shadows* (and others') it begins, "Whenever you have need of anything, and better it be when the Moon is full, you shall assemble in some sacred place, there to adore the spirit of Me, who is queen of all the Witches..."

4. Sanchez, Carol Lee, "New World Tribal Communities: an Alternative Approach for Recreating Egalitarian Societies," *Weaving the Visions: New Patterns in Feminist Spirituality*, ed. Judith Plaskow and Carol Christ (San Francisco: Harper San Francisco, 1989), 344.

5. Ibid, 253.

6. The Wiccan Rede is shorter and easier than the Equal Rights Amendment: "An [if] ye harm none, do as ye will."

7. This is not as peculiar as it sounds. Remember being told that you have to study the whole book because you didn't know which chapters the test would cover?

8. Farrar and Farrar, *A Witches Bible Compleat, Vol. Two*, 17. "Dread" means awesome, not evil.

9. Daniel C. Noel, "A Neo-Jungian Perspective on Neoshaman-ism's Inner Journey," *Witchcraft Today, Vol. 3, Witchcraft and Shamanism,* ed. Chas S. Clifton. (St. Paul, Minnesota: Llewellyn, 1994), 136

10. "Beyond the ordinary"? Yes, the same way that infrared and ultraviolet are beyond the spectrum we can see.

11. Reading the abbreviation for high priest (HP) for the first time several years ago, a young Witch a few weeks into her studies asked whether HP meant "hokey pokey;" so in the southern Arizona Wiccan community this is a long-used and not disrespectful reference to magical and related celebratory activities.

12. We say it this way in reverent jest because there's a verse of "Old Time Religion" that goes like this: "Let us pray with those ol' Druids/as they drink fermented fluids/dancin' naked through the woo-ids/that's good enough for me!"

13. Taking its name from a Nahuatl word for tailfeather. In the Mexican quarter of the Otherworld, the quetzal is a feathered serpent.

14. Lester C. Thurow, *The Zero-Sum Society: Distribution and the Possibilities for Economic Change* (New York: Basic Books, 1980), 11.

15. Jean Shinoda Bolen, *Ring of Power* (San Francisco: Harper San Francisco, 1992), 198.

16. This phrase is part of most rites and blessings in Campsight's *Book of Shadows.*

17. Farrar and Farrar, 17.

18. Although this term technically refers to an element of Australian aborigine religious culture, broad New Age usage of the term has widened its popular meaning to the mythical prehistoric period in any culture's ancestry.

19. Bolen, 216.

20. "The world seemed small to those who believed they could transform it." Margaret Aston, *The Fifteenth Century: the Prospect of Europe* (New York: W. W. Norton, 1968), 65.

21. Don't panic: everything anybody does anywhere changes everything everywhere. In all the metaphors, it's supposed to.

About the Author

Ashleen O'Gaea lives between the worlds, sharing Pax the
Wunder House with her spouse, Canyondancer; their son,
Questor; three cats and uncounted garden wildlives. From
their covenstead in Tucson, she and 'dancer lead Campsight's
sabbat adventures in the southeastern Arizona woo-ids.

Working Magic for Non-Pagans:

The Witch as Magical Technician

By Paul Suliin

Throughout history, every culture has had its magicians. These men and women might work secretly or openly, to help or to harm those around them, depending on their ethics and the laws of their societies. The rewards for their services might be food given in trade, gold from a grateful prince, or death at an Inquisitorial stake. They have been called witches, wizards, seers, *juju* women, *obeahs,* medicine men, alchemists, and astrologers, but when they granted their services to others they all became magical technicians: the doctors, psychologists, meteorologists, and repairmen of their day and age.

Today there are few magical technicians, and fewer still operate openly. There are "fortune tellers" who read cards for their clients and may offer to lift real or imagined curses for ms of money. Police agencies are often suspicious of such servicepeople, and with some reason, for some really are involved in fraud or extortion. Some more ethical psychics and card readers operate in nearly every large city, and there are traditional ethnic sorcerers, such as the *curanderos* of many Latin American societies. Also, there are the Witches and magicians of the modern occult revival.

The tradition of the Witch as magical technician is old and strong, and sooner or later most Wiccans who are out of the closet even with friends and family can expect to be asked to provide magical assistance of some sort, even as simple as a Tarot reading. If you have ever read the Tarot for a friend, worked a healing for someone in need, or blessed a marriage, then you are a magical technician, even if you do not think of yourself that way.

Magical work may be the only contact some non-Pagans ever have with the Craft, and so this chapter will explore some of the more important aspects of this sort of work, and offer advice on how best to answer the needs of those who ask you for help.

Some Pagans feel that magical work for non-Pagans is not a good idea in most cases. There are several reasons given, such as concerns about privacy, ethical problems, and the wish for Wicca to be seen as a religion rather than the usual hex-casting stereotypes.

I do not find these to be insurmountable problems. It is true that many Wiccans do not feel free to "hang out a shingle" and start advertising their services, but I do not know that this is really necessary anyway. The best approach, I find, is to stick close to home and to help those you know and who know you.

Ethical problems have to be addressed on a case-by-case basis. The most common difficulty is a client who wants something from you that you cannot ethically provide, such as a love spell or even a curse on an enemy. Another question is whether or not to take money for your work. I will get into the ethics of magical work a little later and address these sorts of situations, but such special cases are not a barrier to doing magical work for others in general. If someone is prohibited by oath from doing this sort of thing, then there is nothing to be done, but such prohibitions are extremely rare in the types of initiatory oaths and proscriptions I know.

The final issue, that of encouraging people to see Witches as members of a religion rather than purveyors of potions and Voodoo dolls, is among the most delicate problems facing the "working" Pagan. One solution, in my experience, is not to charge for your services. This is not a problem if you do not want to make a business of this, and few of us do. Another help is to look for non-magical solutions to problems. I will discuss this at more length later, but remember that even for a magical technician a spell is not always the best way through every situation.

Why do people seek out magicians? Usually it is because they have a problem that cannot be solved by ordinary means, or at least one that they think cannot be solved that way. It may be because they want a divination to help them with an important decision, or they want to find a lover, or recover something that has been lost, or simply break a string of bad luck. I have been asked to help with problems ranging from healing a sick cat to cleansing a haunted house, from lifting a perceived "curse" to helping a woman deal with her mother's impending death. People I know have helped friends and relatives say goodbye to a lover who had passed away, find homes and jobs, and bless cars and houses.

Broadly speaking, magical work for others falls into the same classes as the sorts of work we do for ourselves. Some common categories are discussed below.

Love Spells

I do not know any public Pagan who has not been asked for one of these. The common fairy tales about Witches so often seem to involve a love charm somewhere along the line. Often the client has a specific person in mind for the enchantment, but this raises some thorny ethical problems for the magical technician. Most interpretations of "harm none," the Wiccan Rede, hold that "harm" includes any form of persuasion that violates another person's free will. It is one thing to help make a person more attractive to potential mates, but most Wiccans draw the line at forcing one person to love another by means of magic (if indeed love can be forced by any means).

I usually handle this first by sitting down and talking with the person requesting the spell. I explain why I have a problem with this sort of magic, and I suggest alternatives, usually a spell to help them find and draw the ideal mate for them. This type of spell names no specific person, and is designed to forge a relationship that is beneficial for all concerned, not a violation of the Rede.

Money Spells

Love may be number one, but money has to be right up there. Money spells can vary quite a bit, from general spells to attract money (which may work out as anything from a sudden inheritance to a raise), to a specific spell to help find a job or win the lottery (not one I recommend myself controlled coincidence can only stretch so far).

Healing

"Witches Heal" is an oft-seen Pagan motto, and it is true: one of the most common tasks for Wiccan magic is healing. There are pitfalls, however, in performing healing magic for others. Most especially, be careful not to fall afoul of your state, provincial, or other laws regarding medical practitioners. First of all, be very, very careful about charging money for a healing—it can open you to charges of malpractice, just like a medical doctor. Also be cautious about giving "diagnoses" or prescribing any form of treatment (magical or otherwise) for a specific illness. That can be considered "practicing medicine," and it can land you in jail unless you are licensed.

This is also a good place to say a word or two about magical herbalism. Herbal cures were the traditional witch's stock in trade, and herbalism is a large part of many modern Wiccan traditions. Nevertheless, all of the cautions about magical healing apply to herbal practice as well, only more so; a healing spell is unlikely to "turn bad" and hurt your client. Herbal medicine, however, carelessly or ineptly applied, can cause active and lasting harm. This is not a business for amateurs, and if you are seriously considering the practice of herbal medicine I strongly encourage you to get professional training. Check your local community; many areas have schools of herbalism that offer training to the public.

After all this it may sound as if there is not much left to be done in the area of magical healing. Unfortunately that is pretty much the case, unless you are very careful in choosing your subjects and your methods. A very general spell for good health and well-being is probably safe, but remember that general spells can have unpredictable results.

A good case in point is a magical working that I did with my own coven some years ago. A close friend of mine named Barbara was dying from inoperable cancer. The coven I work with here in Southern California did a general working for Barb, giving her healing energy to work with as her body best felt it should. Barb died a few weeks later, though she reported that her pain eased considerably immediately after our working, and remained at ease for sometime thereafter.

Did our spell kill Barbara? I do not think so, but neither did it keep her alive. As spells are wont to do, it took the path of least resistance to manifestation, and so it eased her pain as she died. That itself is no small accomplishment, and Barb was prepared for and had accepted her death; making it easier was probably all we could have done.

Protection

Protection spells in general are designed to give the recipient a measure of warding against harm. I have found that making a spell more specific usually gives it more force, and so I think it is good to make a protection spell as specific as possible. Try to determine what sort of harm your client is most concerned about and construct the spell accordingly. For example, if s/he is about to take a trip by air and is concerned about safety, then a spell invoking Hermes as the patron of travelers and flight might be most appropriate. My wife uses a visualization of Anubis and Horus as guardians for our car against thieves and accidents. If your client's concerns are extremely vague or general, a blessing might be more appropriate than a specific spell of protection.

Blessings

This is another traditional role of the Witch. A blessing is a special invocation of good fortune and favor. It is a way of making good wishes concrete. Wishing someone luck is a very simple and general form of blessing, and this class of spell has a lot of room for variation.

A blessing might be a spell to help the success of a new business venture, or a benediction placed on a newborn child, or a very general spell of protection placed on a person or thing. I find that usually a spell that is not specific will work itself out gradually, in the form of many small coincidences, rather than one grand change as might happen with a more specific working. Blessings are a good example of a deliberate application of this principle. I often incorporate a small blessing into a toast or a greeting. I gave one recently by putting a magical "push" (energy and visualization) behind a toast that I gave at a wedding: "May love and light and laughter follow you all the days of your lives, and may the love you share bring you both as much joy as you have brought to all of us." The traditional Wiccan "Blessed Be" is the perfect "seal" to such a spell.

Bindings

A binding is a specialized sort of protective spell that is meant to restrict the actions of a specific person or group of people. Think of it as a magical "restraining order." Most non-Pagans who approach a magician for help will not have heard of these, so if you think it is appropriate you will want to recommend it yourself.

Bindings are used when a person is acting in ways that are directly harmful to others, and needs to be restrained or enjoined from that sort of behavior. For example, I have seen a binding used to prevent a neighborhood bully from terrorizing the local cats, and I know of a binding ritual that was used to prevent an estranged husband from harassing and abusing his wife during their divorce.

Use this type of spell with care. Restricting anyone's freedom of action is not to be done lightly. See my section on ethics a bit later for some ideas on how to judge when a binding is necessary.

Exorcisms and Cleansings

What's that? Exorcism? Isn't that some sort of demonology thing? Well, not entirely. Technically, an exorcism is any working designed to banish things you do not want to have around. It is a sort of psychic housecleaning, and in fact a lighter and more general version of this type of spell is called a cleansing. The standard ritual that you use to cast a circle probably incorporates elements of cleansing and/or exorcism, as you purify your working area prior to beginning any serious magical operation.

Many Witches cleanse their homes and their working areas on a regular basis, just like they straighten a room. It is a useful operation to clear out the psychic "atmosphere" in an area. The result should be a lighter and more pleasant place to live and work. If a person is feeling depressed or morose, a cleansing might be all they need to get a new perspective on things (and by the way, since a lot of what is dragging them down is their own mental and emotional trash, this is a good spell to involve the client in directly). The common ritual of asperging an area with salt water and incense along with invocations of the elements is a basic cleansing rite and, as I mentioned, your circle-casting ritual probably contains elements that you can adapt.

An exorcism is a more involved and serious operation, used when the atmosphere of a place is severely contaminated. If a room or a house has severe negative connotations for someone, due to an associated emotional trauma or some similar cause, or if it just feels extraordinarily "dirty," then an exorcism may be in order. This is a bigger undertaking, but it needn't be the fire-and-brimstone battle that you might think of from the movies. As a rule of thumb, try a cleansing ritual first. If that does not clear out the area you are trying to purify, then do it again, but this time cast a circle if you have not already, add a good banishing incense, and raise a good store of energy to put into the work. If you have a formal banishing ritual, such as the Lesser Banishing Ritual of the Pentagram, it would be appropriate here. In fact, ceremonial magic has a substantial store of rituals useful for exorcism. If you think you might be doing this sort of work, it wouldn't hurt to read up on ceremonialism, such as the Golden Dawn material.[1]

While we are on this subject, I should mention the concept of demonic possession. Ordinarily you might expect to refer someone to the Catholic priest down the road for a problem like this, but that might not be an option right at the time. I was once awakened out of a sound sleep by a phone call from a woman who believed her husband was possessed by a demon. In a situation like this it is best to treat your client gently. Leaving aside for the moment the question of whether or not demon possession actually occurs, the fact is that relatively few people in our society believe that it does, and of those fewer still will admit it. If someone is seriously coming to you with a problem like this, chances are they are pretty upset and on edge. At the very least they need someone to talk to.

I talked to her, and determined to my own satisfaction (and eventually to hers) that what we were dealing with was alcoholism, not possession. As it happened I eventually did refer her to a local minister as well as an alcohol treatment program, because it seemed to me that she needed a religious community more than she needed a magician, and Wicca was clearly not to her taste (she was coming to me in the first place because she thought that as a Witch I would know about demons).

I have never encountered a case of what I would consider true demon possession, but if I did I would probably handle it in much the same way. I would suggest that the client seek a Christian or Jewish religious community and the help of a good therapist. I would do it this way not because I do not trust Wiccan banishing rituals, but because, first of all, the therapeutic approach should be tried first in my opinion—"possession" is often mental illness—and, second, because a person who believes that they are possessed by demons is probably not going to respond well to the ministrations of a Witch. The client's cooperation and willing participation are essential to many magical operations, and it will be easier to get that from within the client's own belief system.

Divination

Many people are interested in knowing the future. I know several Witches who supplement their incomes by providing Tarot readings for the public. In fact you will find that you need not even identify yourself as a Witch. People who see you working with a deck or who notice it on your bookshelf will often ask for readings. Questions might range from the trivial to the serious—from how they will do on an upcoming school test to whether their marriage will last or a loved one will recover from a serious illness.

There is not much way to go wrong providing divinatory services, but there are a few things of which to be aware. First, know the law in your area. Some municipalities have "fortune-telling" laws that forbid taking money or other goods in exchange for divination. These laws are usually aimed at fraudulent "mediums" who use fortune telling as a scam to defraud or extort money from their clients. However, the law may not make such distinctions, and in that case you will need to be careful not to ask for anything in return for your services. It would be wise to consult a lawyer if you are thinking making this a business.

Another item to be aware of is the need sometimes for counselling clients. Especially if the outcome of the reading is grim, the client may need a fair amount of support and comfort in dealing with the results. I recall a woman who asked me whether her mother would recover from a serious illness. The reading indicated that she would not, that in fact she would soon die. Following that reading I kept in touch with the woman for several weeks, helping her deal with the pain as her mother's condition gradually worsened and she did indeed die. Sometimes the magician's job doesn't end when the reading is over.

Mediumship

Mediumship is essentially the art of providing a conduit for other intelligent entities to communicate through you. Many Wiccan priests and priestesses do this during the rite of Drawing Down the Moon. It is also done in automatic writing, and in some oracular or divinatory work. Some clients will ask this of you, for example in the context of communicating with a dead loved one. John Yohalem wrote in the Pagan journal *Enchanté* about a friend who asked him to help make contact with the friend's lover, who had recently died.[2] John's client wanted to say goodbye. John cast a circle and called the man who had passed on, telling his friend that when he felt his lover's presence, he should offer whatever farewells he had. This is another good example of getting the client involved in the work, about which I will have more to say later.

Casting Curses

I include this section only because many clients seem to expect this sort of thing, and so a word or two about curses seems in order. Z Budapest said once that "a Witch who cannot curse cannot heal," and I have heard Witches who were extremely angry or outraged seriously propose this type of magic. (For example during the Gulf War, when Saddam Hussein poisoned the environment by firing the Kuwaiti oil fields, there was talk of magically working against him.)

I would agree with Budapest, insofar as I think any magician has to understand how this sort of magic works. On its face it is a violation of the Rede, but occasionally, when doing nothing can be construed as harmful just as much as working to oppose something, the Rede provides

little specific guidance. More practically, recall that whatever energy you put forth will return threefold. It has
always seemed to me that the Law of Threefold Return
manifests in part through the fact that we are shaped by the
things we do. Working magic transforms us as it transforms
the world, and curses can linger as a poison in our hearts. I
would encourage anyone considering this sort of work to
think about it very, very carefully, and I cannot imagine a
circumstance when it would be appropriate to do this on
someone else's behalf. I do not advise it for the magical
technician—it will return to you, to your client, and to the
harm of the Craft's reputation.

Special Issues for Magical Technicians

There are some special points that need to be addressed and
understood by anyone who wants to do magical work on
another's behalf—especially if the other is not Pagan. These
range from making sure that you and your client understand
each other to making sure that you do not run afoul of the
law. Remember that in any magical working the Witch has
three clients, not just one; you must work to please your
client, to please yourself, and to please the Gods.

Those who understand the magical world view will
often expect different things when dealing with magic and
magicians than those who do not have our understanding.
When dealing with non-Pagans you can't take these things
for granted. Make sure that you understand what they want
and what they need (these may not be the same things),
and make sure they understand what you can and cannot
do to help them.

The very first thing to do when you're approached for a
magical working is to sit down and talk with your client.

What is their problem, and why are they coming to you? What sorts of expectations do they have? Very often people will have a totally skewed vision of what magic is and how it works. A client might expect a money spell to bring cash in the mail the next day, or expect a love spell to have the woman of his dreams throwing herself at his feet. Once you get clear on what the client wants, then you'll have to decide if you're the person to help.

At this stage your role is going to be more that of a counselor than a magician. In talking to your client, try to determine if a spell is really what they need at all. Ritual can be an uncertain tool, and if the client's needs can be met by more mundane means then that is magic of a sort as well, and far more immediate and predictable than a ritual working.

I recall a young man who came to me once to help get his girlfriend back. He was convinced that family gossip and other outside influences were driving them apart, and he wanted a love spell to get them back together. I talked to him for a while about how his relationship had developed and asked him what specific problems seemed to lie between him and his girlfriend. It began to become clear that their problems were the same sorts of problems that might afflict any relationship—mainly a failure of two people to properly communicate about their real needs and desires, combined with some jealous insecurity on his part. It seemed that her family and friends were encouraging her to leave, but mainly because she was already unhappy.

In the end I told him that magic was not the cure he was seeking. In fact, I explained, I could not help him get his girlfriend back because it was clear that she did not want to come back, and the Craft's ethics do not permit me to interfere in that sort of decision. I recommended that he let her go and focus on developing new relationships and working on some communications skills. He was not happy with what I had to tell but, but I did not perform any magical work for him. I did take some time over the next few months to talk to him about the problems he was having, and I think I managed to help a bit.

This sort of counseling is not at all uncommon for the magical technician, and in fact you may find that you help many more people just by listening to their problems than you do by working in ritual. It may not be a bad idea, if you plan to do a lot of this sort of work, to take a course or two in counseling and social work.

Another common point of misunderstanding is the nature and power of magic. Very often people think that magic is an all-powerful cure. They tend to view it as a crutch rather than a tool. People will ask for a spell to fix a problem, then sit back, thinking that the magic will do all the work, doing nothing to help their own situation. They might even miss the help the spell brings their way, because they do not bother to reach out and take advantage of it. This is often an excuse to avoid responsibility—when the situation fails to improve the failure can be blamed on a faulty spell rather than personal laziness. Even magicians may not be immune to this tendency.

For this reason I always give a brief lecture on the theory and practice of magic whenever I help a non-Pagan with a spell. I explain that the spell works by engaging the conscious and unconscious minds through the use of symbolism, that it requires active interest and participation, and that a spell will work itself out more often than not through coincidence. It may be fairly subtle, I explain, and requires some attention if the results are to be fully realized. I'm reminded of a quote from Gwendolyn Piper, a Pagan writer on the Internet. When a man asked why prayers and magic so often go unanswered, she replied "Most answers aren't heard."

This is one reason why it is valuable to have the client participate in the spell itself whenever possible. Every magical worker I know agrees that involving the client in the spell improves the chances of success. The focus of actually working with the spell, under the magician's direction, greatly increases the client's involvement, and so the effectiveness of the working.

This point is important enough that it is worthwhile to say a word or two about spell design, especially with an eye to crafting rituals and symbols that invite client participation. Take as an example a simple spell for money.

Whenever possible, try to incorporate symbols into the working which are personally meaningful to the client. It helps to explain symbols, such as why you might use a green candle for Venus in a love spell (when the client might expect red), and in fact such esoteric or "mysterious" symbolism can offer a psychological boost to a spell. It is also a good idea to include symbolism that engages the client directly.

On the principle that a specific spell is more successful, ask the client to frame his (assuming a male client) needs as explicitly as possible. In a spell for money, determine just what the money is needed for. On a piece of plain white paper about two inches square, trace the sigil of the client's name on the magic square of Jupiter. (Several good magical texts contain the Jupiter kamea and instructions for its use; Israel Regardie's book *How to Make and Use Talismans*[3] is ᴄᴀᴘᴇᴄⁱⁱⁿⁱⁱy ᴄⁱₑₐᵣ ₐₙd ₛᵢₘₚₗₑ.) Explain to the client that this is to "align" him, as it were, with the forces of increase and prosperity that Jupiter represents. Add other symbols as you feel appropriate, explaining them as well. Then have the client write on the other side of the paper a brief but precise description of what the money is needed for. This should be phrased in the form of an affirmation: "I will receive the money I need to pay for my semester at college," or some similar phrasing. Charge the talisman by casting a working circle, and passing the talisman three times through the smoke of frankincense, with a visualization of the appropriate God-form and the following incantation:

> *Osiris, great lord; Isis, queen of magic;*
> *Bless this amulet to Your will and the*
> *Needs of [client's name], who has asked*
>   *Your help.*
> *Bring the blessings he needs.*
> *As we will, so mote it be.*

(Note: I chose Osiris because I work most closely with the Egyptian Deities. Your preferences may vary. If the invocation of Pagan Gods is troubling to your client, try archangels or saints. A priestess I know has found that this calms some worries.)

Place the talisman in a bowl or jar with the sigil up and the client's declaration down. (Do not worry; he will know it is there even if he cannot see it.) Let him take the jar home, and from that point on he should add spare change, loose bills, whatever he has in his pockets, to the jar at the end of each day. Each time he does so he should visualize himself receiving the benefits of the spell, in whatever form he has declared. As the spell progresses he should also begin looking for opportunities to improve his situation toward his goal. The spell will naturally tend to focus his mind that way; just tell him to keep his eyes open. When the jar is full, the money collected should be sorted and given to a charity of some sort. He can give it to a battered women's shelter, buy food for the homeless, give it to a church, or whatever. This is the sacrifice that he offers the Gods in recognition of Their help to him. That seals the spell and it should work itself out in due course after that, if it has not already. The talisman can be returned to the magician for disposal. (I recommend a brief prayer of thanks, followed by burning the amulet in the incense brazier with a bit of frankincense.)

This is a good general model of spell design for this type of work—a spell that involves the client at each phase of design and implementation. The client's energies will naturally be mobilized and channeled by the spell to give the best chance of success. Similar designs can be used for nearly all the types of workings I discussed in the previous pages.

The Ethics of Spell Casting

The Wiccan Rede instructs us to harm no one, and the Law of Threefold Return explains the universe's exchange policy in such matters. However, specific situations can sometimes make it unclear how to apply the Rede. For example, I know many Pagans who won't do even so much as a healing without the subject's explicit permission, regarding it as an interference in the subject's life, an interference forbidden by the

Rede. That's a good, cautious policy, I think, but at the same time I think it is important not to become so paralyzed by fear of "harming" someone that you can take no action at all—sometimes doing nothing can be harmful as well.

In particular I'm annoyed by people who would take direct physical action to stop a mugger or a child abuser, but who would not cast a binding spell to prevent that sort of behavior in the first place. My simple rule of thumb for judging the ethics of magical action is that anything that is ethical by "mundane" means is ethical by magical means. If you would be willing to intervene physically in a dangerous situation to save a life, then you should be willing to intervene magically as well. If you would balk at drugging a woman for sex, then you should be just as unwilling to cast a love spell to bring her to you. This basic rule can help you apply the Rede to many situations. If a client wants you to cast a spell for a particular purpose, ask yourself if you would work for that purpose with your own two hands. If the answer is no, then either help your client find another way, or decline to help him at all.

After all, helping the client should be the overall goal—that is your service to the Gods for the understanding They have given you. That's one reason why I do not recommend taking money for magic; it is too easy to focus on the fee rather than focussing on the client's needs. That concern for the client is also another reason to be careful of your ethics. It is important that the client understand what the spell can and cannot do, so he or she goes into this with eyes open, without unrealistic expectations. Likewise, remember that you understand this process better than the client does, and so you are in some measure responsible for the means you use in the spell. The Threefold Law will come back to your client as well as to you, and it is not right for you to land him in a situation he did not realize was coming.

The magical technician has responsibilities just as serious as a doctor or other professional: to treat clients fairly and with an eye to their needs. Someone who comes to you for help deserves the best effort you can give, and there is a certain satisfaction in rendering that service well.

Notes

1. For example, Israel Regardie's *The Golden Dawn* or Donald Michael Kraig's *Modern Magick*, listed below.

2. John Yohalem, "Daily Life of a Witch," *Enchanté 16* (Samhain and Thesmophoria, 1993), 1.

3. Israel Regardie, *How to Make and Use Talismans* (St. Paul, Minnesota: Llewellyn Publications, 1983).

Suggestions for Further Reading

Amber K, *True Magic: A Beginner's Guide* (St. Paul, Minnesota: Llewellyn Publications, 1991). This is a good basic introduction to ritual design and magical theory.

Donald Michael Kraig, *Modern Magick: Eleven Lessons in the High Magickal Arts* (St. Paul, Minnesota: Llewellyn Publications, 1988).

Israel Regardie, *How to Make and Use Talismans* (St. Paul, Minnesota: Llewellyn Publications, 1983). Here are some practical guidelines to symbol design and the construction of talismans.

——, *The Golden Dawn* (St. Paul, Minnesota: Llewellyn Publications, 1989).

Starhawk, *The Spiral Dance* (San Francisco: Harper & Row, 1979). Another introduction to magic from the Pagan perspective. Also contains much valuable material on ethics and religious practice. This book should be on every Witch's shelf

About the Author

Paul Suliin works as a chemist. He lives in Southern California with his wife Michele and their trained attack cats, Simon and Little Bit. He operates the Los Angeles Area Pagan Information Line and may be reached there at 310-719-9097 or by e-mail (besnode@earthlink.net).

Priestess and Pastor:

Serving Between the Worlds

by Reverend B

I raise my arms in greeting and invocation: "Shining One! Child of light and love! Winter-born King! Bearer of good news to the darkened world! We welcome your return! Be present with us now!" For an instant, I am lost in the magic of the moment. I struggle to remember where I am.

Do I stand before a Pagan altar, surrounded by twelve expectant women and men dressed in long robes, to invoke the Lord of the Winter Solstice? Is it the earth-born sun reflecting on the high mountain peaks that I welcome—or am I raising my arms before a circle of early-morning Christians who have gathered to celebrate the birth of the Christ Child? As I open my eyes, will there be fifty worshippers in Sunday dress, standing in the soft morning glow of a stained-glass chapel? Is it the Sun or the Son that I call? Will the closing words be "Amen" or "Blessed Be?"

It has come to pass in my life that I minister in the ancient tradition of the Celtic priest who leapt the Beltane fires on Saturday night and led the congregation in the Mass on Sunday morning. I am both Pagan priestess and Christian pastor. I serve between the worlds.

Almost fifteen years ago, I was led by my spiritual director, a Jungian psychologist, through a series of dreams and waking meditations to a crystal cave. Assigned to explore this offering from the inner planes in my outer world, I started on the most exciting spiritual journey of my life. I discovered a new religion that would become the anchor of my personal practice and that would shift, enrich, and expand my understanding of my ministerial calling.

As a high priestess of Wicca and an ordained minister in a mainline Protestant church, I have fulfilled my Gemini nature as only someone with Sun, Moon, and three planets in that sign could. The archetype of the lovers, the "sacred marriage," the union of apparent opposites, dominates my mundane life, my spiritual practice, my profession, and my being. Happily, this marriage of Paganism and Christianity has been one mostly "made in heaven"—as above, so below. Integrating these seemingly disparate approaches within my own life and work has proved to be a energizing adventure, with blessedly little tension or conflict.

I was lucky to come to this match with several important factors working in its favor. I was raised in a loving home by parents who, on some unspoken level, had already found a way to blend their own distinct spiritual leanings. During my childhood, we went to a liberal Protestant church every Sunday morning after having spent Saturday afternoon flyfishing in rivers and streams. Somehow, I got the impression that both of these experiences were of a religious nature, to be honored for the insight into the Sacred that they offered.

I was also fortunate to be exposed to world mythology at an early age. I romped with King Arthur and Robin Hood in the English woods of my imagination. I played "dress-up," creating myself into the various Greek gods and goddesses found in the stories read to me by my parents. Along with Mother Goose and Grimm's fairy tales, I learned African, Norse, and Hindu myths.

When I finally stumbled onto the work of Joseph Campbell, years later at the Esalen Institute in California, I was already convinced of the similarities of sacred stories across the planet. I was also more than ready to discover a religion that drew upon the rich images of the world's pantheons. What a treasure house of spiritual stimulation!

In college, my studies in literature filled me with the deep yearnings of the English romanticists, Eastern philosophers, American transcendentalists, and Christian mystics. All of these poured into the cauldron of my soul and brewed up a tasty inner life, which had outer expression in only traditional forms. I was still a regular attender of Christian worship. Religious ferment had not yet taken hold in America, so it was all I knew.

After working for a number of years as an English teacher, I became aware that I was always focusing on the spiritual themes and symbols in my classes. It made no difference to me if we were reading Native American poetry, Russian novels, or excerpts from the Upanishads, I found the religious and mythological aspects most stimulating. I thought: wouldn't it be great to work with these ideas all the time? Would there be some way I could use my knowledge and skills in the field of religion? Therefore, I made the choice to do some graduate work in a seminary.

Deciding to actually pursue ministry on a full-time basis was the result of a clear sense of being "called." When I determined that I would pursue third-degree initiation in Wicca, I also knew I had been called. How could this happen? Who could possibly believe these two seemingly opposite messages? Surely I misheard. I, for one, was completely surprised that I would go into the ministry of any religion at all. I'm not the "type."

As part of entering Christian ministry, I was required many times to express the nature and content of my call. I do not ever remember being asked such a question by my Pagan teachers, but I have pondered the issue from that point of view. To verbalize about such a vocation is most difficult; to explain how I feel drawn to be both pastor and priestess has been one of the great challenges of my life's journey.

To respond to the "how-could-this-have-happened" question, I find help in a recent article in *Parabola* magazine:

> *Each time we experience a sacred call, we are instantly drawn into our true nature. ...The sacred call is transformative. It is an invitation to our souls, a mysterious voice reverberating within, a tug on our hearts that can neither be ignored or denied. ...When such a call occurs and we hear it—really hear it—our shift to higher consciousness is assured.*"[1]

The editors of *Parabola* note in their introductory comments, "This dialogue, a call and a response that takes place between above and below, between inner and outer, between the spiritual and natural world, is basic to every tradition."[2] I truly believe that I have received a "basic" call from a "mysterious voice." It is not Jesus, or Hecate, or Isis who summons me, but Something more fundamental and primal. It is the Divine Mystery, beyond all concrete manifestations, who asks me to serve in whatever path is opened for ministry. I know I am being true to this Voice as my understanding of the Mystery expands.

When I finally decided to go into ministry full-time, only about ten percent of those studying to become clergy were women. In my denomination, women were still pioneers in that field. Already, however, they were making a difference. During my seminary training, both male and female professors introduced me to the feminist critique of patriarchal religion and to the reformist practices that stemmed from them. I read *Beyond God the Father* by Mary Daly and Sheila Collin's book, *A Different Heaven and Different Earth*. Goddess mythology was emerging from behind the veil of "his-story." I learned about God the Mother, a feminine aspect of the Divine that had relevance for one's personal practice but also for designing Christian worship.

I found no problem in changing images and pronouns in relation to the Divine. My experience of the Sacred had not been anthropomorphic since childhood. Being an early adherent of the women's movement, I had already crusaded for nonsexist language. Within me, there was no conflict. I thought religious ideas were supposed to change. As my spouse has often said to me of himself over the years, "If my theo/alogical ideas don't change in some way every six months, I begin to feel stuck!"

In those years, the women's spirituality movement was in its infancy. Its themes were mostly expressed in the academic writings of feminist theo/alogians on the academic level rather than practiced in actual worship settings. I particularly had no knowledge of alternative experiences taking place outside of Christianity and Judaism. Thus, I remained at the intellectual level on my journey toward spiritual wisdom. I used books to explore these ideas in adult church school classes. I revised liturgy in worship. I suppose I also served as an early model of a clergywoman in the churches that I served. I met with others to improve access of lay women to the power structures of the church and society. My own deep needs were still not being sufficiently met, however, even though my work in ministry was very fulfilling and meaningful.

My mother's impending death took me to the Jungian therapist who started me in a new direction. I had asked her to shepherd me through this traumatic process of loss. It was during the exploration of this issue at its many levels that I found myself at the opening to the crystal cave. I was ready for the next step in my development.

My approach to unpacking the crystal cave vision was to make my first visit to a metaphysical book store where I assumed I would find information on crystals. Not only did I find that, but I also discovered Merlin, the magician, also known to me in my childhood, who was said to lie in a crystal cave, awaiting release into a world who needed him. Clearly, we know who it was awaiting his return—me! I also learned that a lot of spiritual exploration was being facilitated by this and other similar establishments. I met people, saw announcements of events and workshops, and jumped in, like so many others who have been drawn to the Pagan path.

Two other concurrent unfoldings molded my present situation as well. As my mother was in the long process of dying and I was exploring the crystal cave, I had a huge desire to get a dog. Although this is not so unusual for most people, for me it was one of the oddest transformations of attitude I have ever experienced. I did not have a pet in my youth because of allergies. I was also bitten by dogs several times as a small child and was quite uncomfortable with animals in general.

Yet, as one spirit, my mother's, prepared to leave the world, another forced his way into my consciousness and finally into my home. I had heard of familiars. Witches in folk tales had cat companions who aided them in magical ways. Soon, it was my puppy dog who was leading me in my vision quests to the crystal cave and other exotic locations. I still did not know that there were actually practicing Witches who might have familiars.

I began working with the "animal powers." Soon, Merlin's owl appeared along with the magician, and I had an inner spiritual companion as well as a manifest one. My relationship to the natural world changed. I began to understand better the ideas of those poets and mystics I had read in college. I brought to my awareness a deep connection to nature, one that my father had planted in my unconscious many years before. My canine guide continues to lead me each day. He has introduced me to the web of life on many levels. I have learned, through him, to communicate with all those of "fur and feather and scale and skin,"[3] and they have had much to teach me.

This animal connection has opened doors of communication for me with Christians about their own relationship with nature. So many have been surprised to have my pastoral calls and counseling offered at the death of their pets. No one apparently had ever affirmed for them the spiritual nature of relationships with animals. This verified for me that many Christians have deep religious experiences with nature, something I had discounted earlier. This discovery was to serve as a basis for an authentic way of ministering in a Christian community even after my own perspective had metamorphosed.

Early in the process of my mother's dying, a third gift came to me, by way of the creation-centered spirituality movement founded by former Roman Catholic, now Episcopal, priest Matthew Fox. One day my spouse brought home one of his books, *Original Blessing*. Here was a totally different way to view Christianity, not as a sin-focused, body-denying, dogmatic religion, but as one that, in tandem with Eastern and indigenous perspectives, might actually address the needs of the late twentieth-century world in a creative way.

Fox appreciates the sacredness of nature, the diversity of people, the value of the feminine, the positive aspects of darkness as well as light, the richness of mysticism, the importance of social justice, and the blessedness of creation. I immediately ordered the magazine *Creation,* published by the Institute for Creation Spirituality in Oakland. When I read about several week-long workshops offered by his organization, I couldn't wait to sign up. Here could be a way to hold all of these emerging ideas together! This event, for which I registered some months in advance, synchronistically started one week after my mother's death.

The connection of these two happenings is articulated by a poem that I read in a book of nature spirituality poetry, *News of The Universe*. Entitled "Kaddish," it addressed the poet's mother who was dying:

Earth is your mother as you were mine,
    my earth,
my sustenance, my comfort and my strength
and now without you I turn to your mother
and seek from her that I may meet you again
in rock and stone: whisper to the stone,
I love you; whisper to the rock, I found you;
whisper to earth, Mother, I have
    found my mother
and I am safe and always have been.[4]

The greatest gift of this creation spirituality symposium, in addition to its syncretic approach, was my introduction to the person who would become my next mentor, Starhawk. I had signed up for one of her daily workshops, thinking this person to be a Native American. (I did know that there were still practitioners of that "old religion" around.) What a surprise to arrive at the conference, read the description of the leaders' backgrounds, and discover that Starhawk was a Witch, teaching in a Christian-sponsored program!

I have studied extensively with Starhawk over the past ten years. She is the one who stimulated my deep love of circle ritual. It is her thinking and her modeling that has had the most influence on my own spiritual practice. She is the one who made clear the need for magical rituals to be tied to social justice work in the world. Most important for me, however, has been her ability to affirm her own Jewish tradition and to admit her earlier desire to be a rabbi, a calling not available to women in her youthful years. She, as well as Matthew Fox, also "took a lot of heat" from both Pagans and Christians when she decided to accept the invitation to teach at the Institute for Creation Spirituality.

I am particularly moved by her vision of Ritual Hill in her utopian novel, *The Fifth Sacred Thing:*

> *The upper slopes of the hill were dotted with shrines to Goddesses and Gods, ancestors and spirits...They encompassed an eclectic mixture of traditions...Up here, the sun was welcomed at dawn on the Winter Solstice, the shofar was blown to announce the Jewish New Year, gospel music was sung on Easter morning, the call to prayer was chanted five times a day, and at almost any time of the day or night someone sat in silent meditation, counting breaths.*[5]

After lengthy training with Starhawk and with others in my local community, my magical partner/spouse and I were initiated to the third degree of Wicca by a Gardnerian-trained high priestess. Some years earlier, I had received what could be considered the third and highest level of ordination by the Christian denomination that I serve. I also am now a second degree initiate of the Order of Bards, Ovates, and Druids, centered in England. However, none of these experiences has compared to that night when I officially accepted my Wiccan calling to serve as leader in the wider Pagan community.

My partner Bear and I stand at the top of stairs, shifting from one foot to another. The door below creaks and opens; a cloud of incense smoke spirals up at us. I inhale deeply. Is it really so chilly this winter night as we wait on these steps, or do I shiver from anticipation and anxiety?

It is time! Slowly we remove our robes, drop them on the landing and tentatively begin the journey downward. One step after another, we descend into the temple of the Gods. At the entrance, we are met by the one who will guide us through our third-degree initiation. After the purification, I notice that the oil of blessing glistens on my partner's forehead, matching the gold sweat also shining there.

As we enter the hazy, candlelit room, long shadows of other skyclad bodies reflect on the wall facing us. Sparks of fire glint off ritual knives and sacred jewelry. Everything twinkles. My vision blurs as the magic of that "time which is not a time" catches me in its grasp.

Before I stepped into that cast circle, I recall flashing on a scene from some years earlier, when I had approached the Christian altar in front of a thousand clergy and lay people to receive my final ordination as minister and elder of the church. The feeling inside me was similar; then, too, had I known both anticipation and nervousness. Then, it was not so much because of the unknown nature of the initiatory process ahead, for I had witnessed numerous ordinations previously. My anxiety stemmed from the great responsibility facing me as I assumed this calling and professional life. Hundreds of congregants would look to me as their spiritual guide. Little did I know then just how broad my ministry would be.

I also recalled wondering, on that Christian "initiatory" occasion, if my personal eccentricities would be accepted by traditional church members. Even before my Pagan conversion, I had worn lots of jewelry and artsy clothes, not exactly the stereotypical look for a Christian pastor—but I am half Romany (gypsy) by birth, and true to my heritage.

I have always been comforted by the words of my first bishop, who later ordained me. During a personal discussion with him one day early in the ordination process, I observed to him that not only was I not a man, (still the expected sex of a pastor) but also I was not a very conventional women. Giving me a hug, he reassured me by saying: "God has called you, rings and all."

To this day, seventeen years later, I have not had one challenge to my personal style or even the gold pentagram that I wear openly. In fact the opposite is true. One seventy-year-old parishioner recently decided that if her pastor could have on more than one ring, so could she. She now sports four of them.

Many Christians, I have discovered, have the same spiritual longings that I have. They only need to be shown how those experiences are available to them within the tradition they embrace. Christianity turns out not to be as narrow and limiting as I once thought, but one must diligently seek out the truths often hidden by the bureaucracies of the institutions and by the barrage of negativity sent out by the minority fundamentalists.

So it is that I now serve "between the worlds." Many insights, resources, and experiences have enabled me to claim space for myself to work in both communities. I feel most grateful that I have been able to earn my living doing spiritual work in one of them, allowing me to volunteer in the other.

If I step back long enough from the outer forms of both paths, I am able to look deeply into their individual sacred wells. There I have found a beautiful and sustaining underground stream where all wholesome traditions run together and from which, I believe, all emerge. This is the source water of spirituality that nourishes my endeavors. As a student and teacher of these traditions, I have developed an appreciation of the many similarities, as well as an understanding of the differences, all of which has supported my joint ministry.

However, Pagans in particular still ask, "How can you authentically preach and teach Christianity? It is so different from Paganism, and why would you want to do it in the first place?" Sometimes those who ask are as closed as Christian fundamentalists might be, so I seldom answer. To speak of my calling by the Divine to do both ministries would be fruitless, since the products of mystical experiences are never explainable in any rational manner.

Both paths share the archetypes of the dying and rising God and the Earth Mother who births the child of light. The specific details of how these images are manifested provide a stimulating opportunity for comparison and critique. Since neither Christians or Pagans agree among themselves as to how these beliefs and symbols are to be interpreted, I certainly don't worry about it.

The co-opting of Pagan festivals by Christianity has also been a bonus rather than an irritant. This situation has enabled me to understand and focus the basic movement of energies, as well as relate my own Pagan practices, to the church's liturgical year. The wheel turns for both religions—the return of the child of light, spring renewal and resurrection, harvest home festivals, sacrifice and death. Allowing the insights of both paths to enrich the celebration of these holy days has been a great gift.

Western sacred texts, too, give evidence of the Pagan roots of the Judeo-Christian tradition. Vision quests, magical workings, healings, and nature symbolism abound in the Holy Bible, awaiting use in homily and liturgy. I have no doubt that Jesus turned the water into wine, that Moses threw down his staff and it became a snake, or that Elijah lighted the fire of the sacrifice by the power of his invocation. I believe, as the Psalmist says, that the Lord rides upon the wings of the wind. It happens every time I cast a circle and call in the East. I relish the whole book of the Song of Songs; it is perhaps one of the most beautiful renditions of the sacred marriage between the king and the Goddess of the Land I have ever read.

Christian mysticism (Jewish and Islamic as well) has provided me many resources for my tandem ministry, as well as my own mystical practice. As I read Hildegard of Bingen, Meister Eckhardt, and Francis of Assisi, I have discovered ideas and experiences that are also accessed by deep Pagan meditation. Language is inadequate for conveying the experience of uniting with the Mystery. Thus, mystical writing from different traditions sounds much the same; outer forms are of little consequence. Clearly, they tap into the same underground source. Mahatma Gandhi explained this concept in the following way:

> *Even as a tree has a single trunk, but many branches and leaves, so there is one true and perfect Religion, but it becomes many, as it passes through the human medium. The one Religion is beyond all speech.*[6]

Pagan training, interestingly enough, has enabled me to find room in my belief system for some Christian practices and ideas that I once discounted. The divinity of Jesus (and the rest of us), the efficacy of spiritual healing, charismatic possession by the spirit (most evident at drumming circles), the magical act of transubstantiation of the communion elements—all these ideas became more acceptable to me because of my Wiccan perspective. I have also discovered, much to my amazement, that I am a "pentecostal Pagan," a devotee of ecstatic religious experience.

On the other hand, Christian training has proved invaluable to me in providing skills for doing ministry in the Pagan community. Techniques of pastoral counseling, group organizing, working with volunteers, public speaking, and ritual design have been of immense aid. I have been surprised at the similarities in demands placed on me by both Christian institutions and as-yet-uninstitutionalized Paganism. With the exception of managing permanent buildings (which could be a Goddess-send or a horrible headache) and large staffs of clergy and support help, all of my training in Christian ministry has been helpful to my Pagan work.

Pagans are just beginning to grapple with the handicap of having few professionally trained leaders. Good intentions cannot be a replacement for skill if Paganism is to be widely successful. There will be an even greater need for expertise as the religion continues to grow. Leading a small group is very demanding; coordinating outer temples and congregations, in addition to community-wide activities and festivals, requires far more experience and training than most practitioners have. Learning on the job will be more difficult as expectations increase and fewer people have access to elder high priests and priestesses who know the "tricks of the trade." Isaac Bonewits in particular has expressed the view that Pagan clergy must strive for excellence in training and practice. Thus, it is no surprise to me that some leaders across the country are taking classes at liberal Christian seminaries in order to develop both the needed skills and the more widely recognized credentials of their attainment.

I have been somewhat encouraged to continue working with the Christian church by the signs of change I see in individual members and within some denominations. Whether these institutions can cope with the conflicting pressures on them both to change and not to change remains to be seen. It is possible that a new form of Christianity, one that will be helpful for twenty-first-century persons as well as the earth, may emerge. It is happening in some places, under the influence of the ideas of such people as Matthew Fox.

On the other hand, perhaps the reactionaries will triumph, or maybe the whole Christian enterprise is on its way out. Many may cheer, but since the religion is still so influential worldwide and certainly in many individual lives, I hope that gradual, positive change will succeed. Its demise, with nothing to replace it for a good share of the population, could be catastrophic for the wellbeing of the planet. The thought of what could rush into the vacuum created by the death of mainline Christianity horrifies me. There are plenty of religious nuts out there!

Therefore, I allow myself to be heartened by the trickles of green spirituality that have flowed into local churches. Some people are learning earth-healthy religious ideas. They are singing new nature-based songs printed in recently revised hymnals. They are using gender–inclusive liturgies and changing old hierarchical models of leadership. I recently even heard a hymn, origins unknown, entitled, "If Jesus Were A Woman." At least the idea has crossed somebody's mind! Catholic nuns, especially, are creating music and rituals that are nature and feminist-focused.[7] The pope has good reason to be concerned!

Mainline Christian clergy, especially women, are being exposed to Pagan rituals in seminaries, at conferences and in professional journals. Sophia, the Hebrew goddess of wisdom, Kali from the Far East, and White Buffalo Woman have been manifesting in Christian contexts around this country. Even as the fundamentalists, a small percentage of Christians, attempt to hang on to the past loudly and sometimes violently, many others are opening to spirituality, developing new forms of worship and changing ideas about the Divine and the natural world.

In the last church I served, for instance, a group of parishioners expressed the desire for a more contemporary, less formal worship service, to be held early Sunday morning. A "ritual" committee was formed to help design this experience. It was a great surprise to me that the group decided to move the service to the rear of the sanctuary in a large open space, set movable chairs in a circle and put a very Pagan-looking altar at the center. During the years that I facilitated this worship experience, we invoked the Divine in many forms, read poetry and prose from various sources of wisdom, handled many symbolic, sacred objects, chanted, and shared bread and wine in the more celebrational form of standing around the altar, talking and feeding one another. About fifty men and women of all ages participated in this worship experience weekly. I was especially surprised that many older people were attracted. Ministry is always amazing!

One special person, in addition to my spouse, has made it more possible for me to remain working as a "Pagan in Christian clothing." After years of feeling dour and drab in my traditional black robe, I finally commissioned a woman who makes clergy vestments to create for me a purple stole, shining with gold and silver stars of various sizes and shapes. Not only did she design and produce it beautifully, but also when I arrived to pick it up, there, hanging on the rack already made, was another of her originals. Appliqued on a white chasuble was a black wheel divided into four sections. In each was embroidered a tree branch in its spring, summer, fall, and winter manifestation.

As far as I know, this needle artist comes from a solid Christian background and present-day practice. Her creativity, however, must certainly tap into the deeper place from which emerge images that feed Pagan as well as more traditional paths. Her visions have supported my visions and the possibility of holding them together.

We gather for a ritual of remembrance of those who have passed during the last year. Twinkling candles and mesmerizing music transform our consciousness. Before us is a full, green-leafed potted tree, the tree of life, perhaps fifteen feet high. At its base sits a basket holding the fruits of vine and field. In the tree branches are draped long black ribbons. As the ceremony continues, three dancers dressed in white gradually remove the black strips and replace them with ribbons of bright red, which vibrate with life and the vitality of the summer season.

At this moment appears a beautiful and very pregnant woman, her head encircled by a wreath of apple blossoms. In her long white robe, she is the Earth Mother herself, moving the bread and wine from the base of the tree to the center of the altar. She then goes to sit beneath the tree, one hand on its trunk. The Empress card from the Tarot deck has never manifested more eloquently. We are filled with abundance and new life.

I was brought back to ordinary time and place by the sound and movement of hundreds of Christians coming forward to receive Holy Communion. My Pagan spirit was lifted even higher by the knowledge that such a ritual could take place at a major meeting of the denomination I serve, and I didn't have anything to do with its planning. Some things do change!

Earlier in the day, at the beginning of my denomination's meetings, another amazing event occurred. At the opening worship service, attended by the same thousand delegates, a Native American shaman led a very powerful participatory ritual of drumming, calling the directions, and storytelling. The ballroom vibrated with deep spiritual energy. There were no yawns and foot-shuffling in that service!

Unfortunately, not enough things are changing in Christianity. At these same meetings, I sat in shame and sorrow as a few of the other delegates continued seeking ways to reject homosexuals as clergy. I bemoaned the fact that the institution is more concerned about increasing church membership than developing the spiritual lives of those who already attend. I winced when oppressive legislation was brought before the body by a handful of right-wing churches. I also, quite honestly, was bored to death by the tedium of the business.

My struggle to continue working with the Christian church usually becomes much greater as I get closer to the institution and further from individual parishioners. Fortunately, my superiors have mostly left me alone, and local members have never raised one question about the theo/alogy or focus of the spiritual guidance that they receive. This would not be the case, I suspect, if I were "out of the broom closet" with more than just my ideas.

Because I am open about my paid profession in the Pagan community, I have been confronted with questions about my "serving between the worlds." Clearly, the labels "Christian" and "Witch" refer to what appears to be two totally different religions. These terms, to many people, are antithetical. They carry a buggy-load of hostility and suspicion on both sides.

One Wiccan practitioner (who interestingly enough is not "out" either to his family or his workplace) asked what my congregation thought of my being a "Witch." When I said that I don't use such labels in that setting, he accused me of being hypocritical. "How can you mislead them like that?" he asked. I told him that I had grown beyond the age of rebellion, during which we say wild things in order to get a reaction. I also noted that many Christian clergy (as well as Pagan ones) hold vastly different understandings of the religion than their congregants. In terms of integrity, I would never offer anyone perspectives that I cannot both affirm for myself and find solidly grounded in Christian tradition. There is no asset to turning people off, frightening them, disillusioning them, or losing my own job, when I have legitimate and significant pastoring to offer them. Red-flag words such as "Witchcraft" are always not useful.

Another Pagan suggested that I might be leading my parishioners astray, away from the tradition they have chosen. I responded that the goal of both good pastors and priestesses should not be conversion, but helping people to reach spiritual maturity. We must always start "where people are" and help them grow by offering tools for their own self-development.

I do not come from a dualistic background of right and wrong belief. I do not minister in the fundamentalist style of telling either Christians or Pagans what they ought to do. The many forms of both Christianity and Paganism allow for great latitude within one's own chosen path for growth. I work within wings of both traditions that encourage people to discover their own truths rather than follow a "party line." I abhor repressive institutions, uncreative practices, and narrow understandings, wherever they manifest.

However, when I read the articles in the Pagan press, hear the snide remarks made at gatherings, witness the Christian-bashing that is going on in the Pagan community, I am sad. My sadness comes not from a personal hurt, for I no longer identify my ego with that religion, but because it repeats a pattern that Earth can no longer afford—stereotyping of the "other." I am only surprised that I have not yet heard some rabid Pagan proclaiming, "The only good Christian is a dead one!"

Just like most Pagans, I would not want to be held responsible for the negative actions of others in the community, across the planet, or over the centuries. So, too, it is unjust to reject all Christians for what individuals or factions or institutions have done in the name of Christianity.

When I started on the Pagan path, I thought I would find people with whom I had much more in common. They would be egalitarian in relation to gender issues. They would be liberal in their politics and actively working in the mundane as well as magical world in behalf of social justice, peace, and environmentalism. As persons aware of the need for balance and wholeness, and as spiritual practitioners equipped with the tools to make this happen, they would be physically and emotionally healthy. There would be no Pagan fundamentalists, racists, or sexual vampires. Religious wars would be out; tolerance for diversity would be in. Karmic kindness and compassion would actually be practiced.

However, people are people and religions are religions, wherever you find them. Thankfully, some of my idealistic expectations have been met. Many of my Pagan friends and acquaintances practice their religion with integrity. Conversely, some people have made it very clear to me that my expectations of Paganism are wrong. So it is that I still have more in common with some of my Christian parishioners than I do with Pagans. However, I also have more in common with my Pagan friends who practice sacred sex, who dance around the circle in celebration of Mother Earth, and who know the God and Goddess in both themselves and their partners, than I do with Christians who focus on sin, heaven, and right belief.

There are also legitimate differences between Pagans and Christians that cannot be ignored. If these two paths were the same, there would be no Mystery and no human struggle to permeate the veil. Life would certainly be a lot less intriguing, and the enchantment of "not knowing" would be lost.

Having ministered in both Christian and Pagan communities for many years, I have noticed a change taking place within me. I have not inwardly identified myself as a Christian for some time. Interestingly enough, as I continue to learn and grow, to develop my spirituality, I am not so quick to label myself as a Wiccan either. As these two paths, and others, are explored, instead of "diverging into the woods," they seem to be coming together. Out of this melding in the cauldron of my soul, something new is being born, something exciting, stimulating, yet unnamed. The magic of alchemy is afoot! No one path exhausts the truth for me anymore; inspiration, greatness, and limitation are present wherever I look. The Holy springs forth wherever there is an opening!

When it comes right down to it, I guess I agree with Mahatma Gandhi, who observed: "After long study and experience, I have come to these conclusions: that (1) all religions are true, (2) all religions have some error in them, (3) all religions are almost as dear to me as my own."[8]

I recently heard spiritual artist and writer Meinrad Craighead speak. A painter of much depth and symbolic richness, she apparently is often asked if, in light of her "pagan" insights and her Catholic upbringing, she still believes in God the Father. "Oh, yes! I believe in God the Father, but that's not all I believe. I believe in the richness and diversity of many manifestations of the Divine that emerge from the common pool. I assume the truth to be located beneath all worlds."

In reading the extensive literature analyzing the present-day development of culture and religion, the concept of paradigm shift appears again and again. Old ways are breaking down; new models and myths have yet to emerge. As scholar of comparative religions Joseph Campbell remarked many times, we seem to stand at a crossroads where the "already" and the "not yet" interact. Where the road leads is still hidden from view.[9]

All the old ways—especially the dualistic, we-have-all-the-answers ways—whether Christian or Pagan, are changing as they mix and match in the collective mind and in my depths as well. I suspect that I am but a microcosm of the greater revolution in consciousness, as reflected in my need to move beyond tribalism, both Christian and Pagan. I may be experiencing what the planet needs, a way to hold together more than one perspective on the truth. Fur and feather, scale and skin, leaf and mountain blend as the web of life is being respun—and Mystery looms large on the horizon.

"Shining One! Child of light and love! Winter-born King!" Once again I am caught in that magical moment between the worlds. In this season when Pagans, Christians, Jews, and untold others celebrate the festival of the returning light, I reflect on my own rich spiritual practice.

Although I'm not much into the "biggest buying season of the year," neither am I a "let's-keep-Christ-in-Christmas" adherent, nor "let's-reclaim-the-Pagan-holiday-those-nasty-Christians-stole-from-us" advocate. I find that there is enough to the Spirit to go around for all who honor the cycles of the soul. So, in my own way, I seek to "keep the meaning of the season."

Mostly, I love the glitz of this winter holiday. I put on my gold embroidered robe, decorate a tree with hundreds of twinkling lights, ignite the candles on the altar and do lots of sympathetic magic to lure the light back into being. I feel connected to the energy that runs through all of the traditions. It really doesn't matter to me if it's at a Pagan altar on a mountain top or in a sun-dappled Christian chapel in the city. That's what so special about honoring all these holy days that fit together as spokes on the great wheel of the Divine. Christmas trees, Yule logs, Hanukkah bushes—everyone inherently understands that we need the promise of greenness, of new life, in the midst of winter.

As the poet Robert Frost put so eloquently, "We dance around in a ring and suppose. But the Secret sits in the middle and knows."[10] Blessed be the Secret in all its diversity. May we come to know it in all its fullness!

Notes

1. David Lamborn Wilson, "Invitation to the Soul," *Parabola* (Spring 1994), 9–11.

2. Editors, "Focus," *Parabola* (Spring 1994), 3.

3. From the song, "Fur and Feather" found on the cassette tape *Branches,* by Kenny & Tzipora.

4. David Ignatow, "Kaddish," in *News of the Universe*, ed. Robert Bly (San Francisco: Sierra Club Books, 1980), 178.

5. Starhawk, *The Fifth Sacred Thing* (New York: Bantam Books, 1993), 11.

6. Glyn Richards, *The Philosophy of Gandhi* (London: Curzon Press Ltd., 1982), 18.

7. An example of this is Miriam Therese Winter's book and tape, *Woman Prayer Woman Song* (Oak Park, Illinois: Meyer Stone Books, 1987.)

8. Dhirendra Mohan Datta, *The Philosophy of Mahatma Gandhi* (Madison: University of Wisconsin Press, 1953), 45.

9. Joseph Campbell, *The Power of Myth* (New York: Doubleday, 1988), 31–32.

10. Robert Frost, "The Secret Sits," *Complete Poems of Robert Frost* (New York: Henry Holt and Company, 1949) 495.

About the Author

Reverend B is an ordained minister in a mainline Protestant denomination and has served as a local church pastor for fifteen years. She has a doctorate in religious studies and has taught at various colleges and universities. She lives in a Western city with a large and active Pagan community, which she serves as ritualist and teacher. Her own coven, Kronies' Grove, is composed of eleven men and women, all over the age of fifty. She is a charter member of the Women's Spiritual Leadership Alliance, a philanthropic, educational, and support organization for Wiccan priestesses. She is also a regular participant and teacher at various Pagan festivals around the United States and a member of a working ceremonial magical lodge.

Coming Out of the Closet:

Is it Always Necessary?

by Morven (of *Harvest*)

Although I edited a Pagan/Wiccan publication[1] for more than ten years, I was not public at work about my beliefs and have an entire group of work-related friends who know nothing about my belief system or the extent of my involvement in the Craft. Many Pagan jaws drop at hearing this; more will drop when I say that being in the closet can be good.

Being in the closet is not always the politically correct choice these days. There are many who feel we must be out to show people we aren't murdering babies and eating them. However, those of us old enough to remember the Peace Movement remember the phrase "working within the establishment." I think many modern-day Wiccans have forgotten the value in that. Closeted Wiccans have an important role to play, as do public Wiccans. There is a need for both the closeted Wiccan and the public Wiccan. The two roles are necessary and can be complementary.

I may ruffle a few feathers, anger a few hearts. You are probably expecting me to say I welcome such controversy, that I feel there is nothing like a good argument. Nothing could be further from the truth. I hate the bickering that divides our community. Back when I was editor of *Harvest,* I printed many a controversial letter or article, encouraged to do so by people who wanted frank, honest, discussion. I soon found, however, that people got so caught up in the art of debate and verbal riposte that they forgot what their original intent was: to share thoughts, ideas, ideals—and in the meantime, yours truly got caught in the crossfire.

Apparently I was not the only one. I saw more and more Pagan and Wiccan publications go through the same round, from a timid beginning to a daring dash of controversy to "let's not print anything that will offend anyone." I still don't like the idea of offending people. However, I would like to be able to suggest things you might not have heard, and I am still naive enough to believe that people can listen to new ideas and argue different points of view with both intelligence and respect.

That being said, since many in our community feel that closeted Witches do the Craft a disservice, I humbly submit the other side of the story.

Why Stay "In the Closet"?

Gays called it "being in the closet." Some Witches call it "being in the broom closet." Whatever you call it, some choose to stay in, some widely fling open the doors, crying, "I'll hide no longer in the dark! I am what I am, and I am proud of who I am!" Yet there are sometimes compelling reasons to stay secretive about lifestyle choices or religion.

Sometimes your religious choice causes only mild distur-
bances in your community but, as John Yohalem wrote in a
1993 issue of *Tides,* "If we're going to insist on using this
word [Witch], we'll better be ready to accept and deal with
all the response the word excites. People are going to think
we're silly. People are going to think we're imaginary. People
will say we're in league with the devil, and it's no use telling
them there isn't one if they've been raised to think there is
and that he has horns and hooves and is rampantly sexual
out in the woods, and there we are."[2] Though some may just
look down on you, the response can be more intense.
According to Amber K, author of *True Magick,* "Reactions
from neighbors may run the gamut from 'Isn't that, er,
quaint!' to 'Definitely a mental problem!' to 'Devil-worship-
per!' It is quite possible that one could lose a job, have property vandalized, or even be physically attacked for practicing
magick, even in the 'enlightened' Western civilizations."[3]

If it is bad when people do not believe that we're real, it's
often worse when they do. As an English friend of Gerald B.
Gardner once said, "If it were known in the village what I
am, every time anyone's chicken died, every time a child
became sick, I should be blamed. Witchcraft doesn't pay for
broken windows!"[4] Yes, fanatics and bigots may harass you,
may damage your property and even threaten your life. Illegal, you say? Morally wrong? Did that ever stop the Klu
Klux Klan? Did that stop Hitler? In his book *Sociology,* Paul
Landis wrote, "Throughout history religious reformers and
members of new religious sects have often paid for their
faith with torture and death—the Christians in early Rome,
the leaders of the Reformation in Europe in the sixteenth
century, and the Catholics in England less than a century

later."[5] Even old religions suffer. "During a large part of their history as a religious people the Jews have been bitterly prosecuted."[6]

Job Considerations

Some would say that claims of violence or even just job discrimination against Witches are exaggerations. Fritz Muntean says, "There is a widely held belief among members of the Craft that 'real-name exposure' will cause a Pagan to lose his or her job, have crosses burned on the front lawn, etc. I have been a Pagan for almost twenty-five years, and although I have heard many horrific stories (mostly third- and fourth-hand), I have never personally known anyone who has lost their job, had crosses burned, etc. because their real name was uttered or published by a fellow Pagan!"[7] He goes on to say that most of the loss-of-job stories were either ones where the job loss had "nothing at all to do with the issue of 'real-name exposure' by others," were only part of the story, or were too long ago to be verifiable.

He does have a point there. I cannot think of any people who have lost their job because someone else revealed them as Witches. I can, however, name four people who lost their jobs within a two- to three-year span after they had revealed *themselves* as Witches. Even Valerie Voigt, who says, "In the end most Pagans must come 'out of the broom closet' if we are to survive," adds that being open about her religion at work has sometimes "made people uncomfortable and in at least one case it got me fired."[8]

In any of these cases, was their job loss directly related to their Craft involvement? Who knows? Job loss for discriminatory reasons is always hard to prove. Who among us is always perfect at their job? In any given week, we make mistakes. We might be a few minutes late coming in or returning from break, we might make a personal call on company time, and so on. Normally these minor transgressions are overlooked. When you announce yourself as a Witch, though, you make yourself different from those around you. Suddenly you are not part of the "family" anymore, and minor transgressions are not as easily overlooked.

Perhaps because you are a Witch and a healer, people start spending a lot more time in your office asking for help. Suddenly you are not able to complete as much work as before. Co-workers get jealous. It takes skill and care to prevent endangering your job in a situation like this. Yes, it can be done, and I know people who have done it well. Does that mean everyone should come out? Is that the only choice for a conscientious Witch?

When you are "out of the broom closet," people sometimes stop seeing you as a person and judge you as a Witch. In other words, instead of saying, "There goes Jane. She knows everything there is to know about doing the monthly trial balance," they may say, "There goes Jane the Witch." Raises, promotions, staying off the layoff list all depend on you being perceived as good at your job. If all people can think of is that you are a Witch....

Why Come Out?

Some feel that if we are secretive and do not admit we are Witches, then others will think we are hiding something. True. Yet sometimes I think that we could do our rituals in broad daylight in the town square, and it wouldn't prove anything. They would think we were saving the really bad stuff for private. (Didn't they say that about the early Christians?)

Some feel that we are not only hiding things from out-siders, but that we are hiding things from each other. "I agree that it makes me uneasy when I hear someone intro-duce themselves as 'Starbeam,' and I have no idea what their background or training is," wrote Magenta in a 1991 issue of *COG Newsletter.*[9] True, but if I told you my name was Susie Green (or whatever my real name was), would that tell you anything about my background or training? No. The same writer continues, "I am a bit weary of people who say they are leaders of the Craft, and who are known only by an obvious pseudonym. You can't lead very well from a closet." Once again, I respectfully disagree. A Wic-can who chooses a public Wiccan name and sticks with it can lead well using that name.[10] I even bet that many of our leaders are using pseudonyms, even if they sound mundane and not overtly Wiccan.

For many, a very important goal is to help Paganism become a respected part of the mainstream. The participation of Wiccans in the 1994 Parliament of World Religions is an example. In her article in *Tides,* Sarah S. wrote, "Every Pres-byterian or Jew or Catholic who tells their congregation about the Parliament…opens new doorways of under-standing in the world. It is in everyone's interest to help keep these doorways open."[11] They feel the time has come to stop being so isolationist. In a 1991 issue of *COG Newsletter,* Darcie wrote, "I would like to suggest that now is the time to start saying that what we want is not to be left alone, but to be accepted by other religions as legitimate partners in the work that must be done to salvage the envi-ronment and encourage world peace."[12] However, is mak-ing Wicca a "populist movement" the right thing? One might equally well argue that a populist Paganism is fine, but it becomes more of a religion and less of a mystery religion. As Doreen Valiente said, "I feel rather intimidated at the idea of a mainstream religion. I think I would be happier if we were more what old Gerald used to call 'the cult of the twilight divinities.' I mean, on the edge of civilization, away from the mainstream religions."[13]

Could it be that we are getting the religion confused with the practice, that we forget that magick has different needs? Is there, perhaps, a need for a division, for a public, open, practice, and the "cult of the twilight divinities" that reaches further, risks more, shares less?

What About Magick?

So far I have talked about very mundane, earthly things: jobs, neighbors, broken windows. What about magick, and why did I not mention it first?

When I first joined the Craft,[14] magick was not only very real in the Craft, it was a major part of it. In recent years, though, I have met people who identify themselves as Witches who do not practice magick. One told one of my coveners, "I don't believe in the supernatural." To be fair, maybe what she really meant is that she does not think of magick as supernatural, but that was not the first time I heard of people who worship the Goddess and honor the seasons, yet stop short of spells, rituals to bring results, and so on. Although I am happy to see the Goddess get her due and glad to see some of the excessive use of magickal power wane, I disagree that Witches do not practice magick, and it is odd for me to hear someone call herself a Witch and say she does not believe in the supernatural. I still believe in and practice magick, and I try to teach my students to do the same—responsibly.

One segment in our First Degree training concerns what has been called The Witches' Pyramid. As described by Amber K in *True Magick,* the four sides of this pyramid are "a creative imagination, a will of steel, a living faith, and the ability to keep silent."[15] Secrecy is part of the magickal tradition. I've already mentioned the first need for secrecy: that of protecting oneself. (As Lú put it in his article for *K.A.M., A Journal of Traditional Wicca:* "Cats that show their claws too much get tossed across the room. This is a Christian country."[16])

Another reason for secrecy is the old occult maxim, quoted by Paul Huson in *Mastering Witchcraft: A Practical Guide for Witches, Warlocks, and Covens,* that "Power shared is power lost."[17] That is, when you talk about something, you dissipate its power. That is one reason why talking things out is so important in interpersonal dynamics—by talking about strong emotions like anger, you dissipate them. Talking about spells, rituals, and so on, however, "reopens the issue; the subconscious minds of those involved will silently hand back the unresolved work order to the conscious mind for alteration,"[18] according to Lú. That is, talking about magick brings it back to the conscious mind. The conscious mind is not where magick happens; the subconscious is. Talking about magick you've performed brings it out of the sphere of action to a place where it is not very well-suited.

Talking about Witchcraft in general may seem different from talking about specific acts of magick and may actually be different, but one of the other cornerstones is will. Will requires a strong belief. It is hard to work up energy and magickal passion for day-to-day things; talk about Witchcraft constantly and it becomes too mundane. There is a fine line between living your beliefs and making Witchcraft too commonplace to evoke power. Yes, some can live their beliefs, and find that living it daily increases their power but can we all? Do not the exotic parts of magick act as triggers for some of us?

Also, can you keep up your will of steel, your living faith, in the face of disbelievers who mock you with "You don't believe that, do you?" or "It's just coincidence," or even the simple "Yeah, right" with a disdainful rolling of the eyes? If you decide to be open about your involvement in Witchcraft, make sure your faith in your abilities is strong before you start announcing yourself to the world. "My faith in the Gods is strong enough!" you say. That's fine. However, I am not talking about your faith in the Gods; I am talking about your faith in yourself and in your own abilities. Remember that I am talking about practicing magick. To do so requires a faith in oneself just as much as a faith in the Gods.[19]

In *Applied Magic,* Dion Fortune describes the important task of forming a group mind. "[T]he Group Mind is built up out of the contributions of many individualized consciousnesses concentrating on the same idea."[20] This group mind, once formed, has its own momentum, amplifying the power of single individuals or even of a loose group. "What could be more conducive," asks Fortune, "to the formation of a powerful group mind than the secrecy, the special costume, the processions and chantings of an occult ritual?"[21]

Talking about Witchcraft has another possible bad effect. Many Witches and magicians believe in thoughtforms, or collections of energy. When you talk about Witchcraft in front of someone who is unsympathetic, their thoughts of anger, hatred, fear, and so on collect in a thoughtform of negative energy that can attach itself to you, unless you are magickally vigilant and sophisticated enough to set up protection against this energy.

When you talk about Witchcraft in front of a stranger who may be a Witch, there is always the possibility he or she is jealous, immature, or unethical. Your open sharing could be misconstrued as bragging. As Fortune explains, "Bragging is always a dinner bell to those who feed on miseries; they'll feel a little better about their lowly state when they've dragged you down to join them." I am not saying they would consciously cast a spell against you. Remember those thoughtforms I mentioned? What is most likely is that this poorly developed soul will sit there and stew and simmer, the person's jealousy and envy forming into one large astral black cloud, tenaciously attaching itself to you even as you speak.

Some of the more altruistic Witches will notice that I have focused on some very selfish things—risks to self, loss of personal power. Are we not told, "Thou must suffer to learn?" Well, yes, but we suffer enough in just applying ourselves to our studies, making sacrifices of our time. Martyrs are part of the mythology of other religions, but, as far as I know, not a part of ours. Martyrs are not something that our religion requires us to emulate.

A Moral Obligation

Some feel that we have a moral obligation to explain, reclaim, and defend our faith—that we have to honor the memory of the millions who died because they were accused of being Witches. Others more qualified than I have argued back that the "nine million" were not really nine million, and of those who died, a very small percentage really were Witches. It is very honorable to make sure the Witches among them did not die in vain, I agree, but is dying for our faith the only way to honor them? We honor our spiritual ancestors best when we keep the Craft alive. We cannot keep it alive if we are not ourselves alive.

You can honor the memory from inside the closet, sometimes even more effectively than from outside the closet. Say you are at work and you are not "out" about your beliefs. The subject of Wicca or Paganism comes up, probably because one of our public brothers or sisters was interviewed in the local paper or on television. You can defend the Craft, and people will listen to you because they think you are one of them. You look like them, you act like them, so they listen. Without public people on the television and radio, the subject would never come up, but without the underground people like you saying, "Gee, I don't think those people are weird. Why do they upset you so much?" we would not get very far. The Goddess needs us both. It takes a large amount of courage to be public and make the personal appearances and put up with the press, but it takes another, subtler courage to worship Her in secret and still maintain that "average" persona.

Let's go back to how a closeted Witch can defend from the closet and in doing so can complement the brave work of her public brothers and sisters. It is Samhain. On almost every television channel, in every newspaper, someone interviews a Witch. Your local news station has featured a very public, very vocal Witch who just happens to wear black robes and look very much the part of the Witch. The lunch table discussion goes something like this:

Co-worker #1: "Hey, did you catch the news last night? What is it with that Hazel Smith?"[22]

You: "Hazel Smith? The name sounds familiar…."

Co-worker #2: "She's the one who claims to be a Witch."

You: "Oh, her. Isn't she the one who organizes all those charity events, like the coat collection for the homeless and the toys for children at Christmas?"

Co-worker #1: "Does she?"

You: "Yeah, and I think she and a bunch of her friends had a big presence in the walk for cancer research last month."

Co-worker #1: "I didn't know that. All I know is she looks so creepy."

You: "Creepy? What's so creepy?"

Co-worker #1: "Well, for one thing, she wears black all the time!"

You: "But nuns and priests wear black—"

(Unfortunately someone makes a snide comment about the news stories lately about Catholic priests and young boys, but you turn the conversation away from that and continue.)

You: "Seriously, though, is that all that bothers you, her clothes?"

From there it goes on to a general discussion of clothes, of rebels, of who wore black when (beatniks, disaffected youth of any age, widows in certain parts of Europe, and so on), and it eventually moves away from your original point of discussion. People leaving the lunchroom probably will not even remember how you got on the subject of clothes, but they will go away with two new thought seeds: that black clothes can mean many different things and that this woman who calls herself a Witch has been a strong supporter of community charities.

If people think you are one of them, they think your values are similar. If, then, you say Witches are not bad, maybe they will listen because, after all, you are a nice person. However, what would happen if co-worker #1 knew you were a Witch? If he were very open-minded, he might ask you if you knew Hazel, and maybe ask you for more information on something she mentioned in her interview. If he were close-minded or had strong anti-Witch feelings (as co-worker #1 seemed to), he might not even sit with you at lunch to begin with. If he did, he probably would not bring up the subject because he would know that you would defend it. Therefore, by being in the closet you have actually facilitated things being brought out in the open, and you have helped people see things differently. In ways like this you can sometimes do more as a member of the "establishment" than as an outsider, and Witches are often considered outsiders.

Making the Decision Yourself

We live in fortunate times right now. Though I have cited friends who were "out" and lost their jobs, there are currently a couple of people in my coven who are "out" and are doing quite well at their jobs. People can wear pentagrams outwardly—at least in some parts of the world—and live to tell the tale. However, if the Burning Times come back again the public Wiccans will need the underground Wiccans to give them shelter, support, and help them regain the ground we have lost.

It is up to each one of us to decide whether we can serve the Goddess and the Craft better underground or out in the open. I cringe when I hear of people "outing" others without their permission. I am a firm believer that there is a real need to have people underground and people out showing that Wiccans are normal people.

The decision to come out of the broom closet, like the decision whether or not to have children, is an extremely personal one that only you can make. Only you can decide if you should come out and to whom.

"A degree of uniformity is necessary if we are to interact comfortably…. Perhaps the most basic of all group norms is 'thou shalt conform'"[23] according to Dennis Coon in his book, *Introduction to Psychology*. The more rigid the norms and need for conformity, the harder it will be for you to come out of the closet. Even among people who do not seem to conform, there are dangers. In a posting on CompuServe's New Age Forum, Rhianna said, "When I lived in California, I had a great many friends who were gay, both male and female. I went to clubs with them, and had a great time. Anyway, finally, I felt comfortable enough to come out to them about being Wiccan and 'Kapow!' You'd have thought they were all 'Bible-thumpers!' To make a long story short, I was accused of devil worship, and hexing people, and was quickly 'excommunicated' from almost all of these friendships. (Needless to say, this story is only amusing after the passage of several years. It wasn't amusing at all back then). I find it interesting that, while I was completely accepting of their 'alternative' lifestyle, they just couldn't handle mine!"[24]

If you decide to come out, read up on the experiences of Pagans and Wiccans who have.[25] Just reading their experiences will help evaluate your situation and will give you strength in whatever you choose.

The Best Laid Plans...

I am not out of the closet at work, but as I have grown older and more confident in my abilities to find a new job if I have to, I have become a little more open about how I love nature and think Goddess worshippers have the right idea (after all, I am a woman, so that makes sense). Among the right group of people, I will even defend Witchcraft with "Some of my friends are Witches...". However, I draw the line at admitting I am Pagan or a Witch. The closest I will come is to say, "Some of my friends are Pagan, and I've got to say I agree with a lot of what they say"—all of which is true. When it comes to the "W" word, though, I stop short because I do not want to waste my time repeatedly explaining who I am and who I am not, then having to make up the time I spent talking to them so I will not lose my job.

One man at work has read *Iron John* and even *Drawing Down the Moon*. He knows I have friends who are interested in science fiction and fantasy, and one day he sat down in my office and said, "Cath[26], ever play Magic?" I was in a puckish mood and said, half under my breath, "No, I work very hard at it." "I know, Cath," he calmly replied, looking me straight in the eye, then, without missing a beat, continued talking about the new fantasy card game called Magic. He finished describing the game, then calmly said, "You know, you've changed my whole idea about Witches." In just a few more short sentences, he let me know I had shown him that they were not evil, that they were good, and that he was glad to have met me.

I mentioned this to my coven, saying, "I should say to him, 'How do you know I'm a Witch? I never said I was a Witch,'" but they suggested I let it lie. That's where it is now: a silent understanding, an unspoken connection. He never called me a Witch, and I never said I was one. Even so, I still think I have met my moral obligation—at least one more person in the world knows we are okay.

I have never done even one television interview. However, he never would have known about my beliefs if someone, somewhere had not. It took two groups of people—public Witches and private ones—and in the end, it worked. Isn't that what really matters?

Notes

1. *Harvest,* which was published from October, 1980 through Fall, 1992.

2. John Yohalem,"Witches and pagans and heathens (Oh My!)," *Tides,* Beltane/Summer Solstice 1993: 41.

3. Amber K, *True Magick* (St. Paul, Minnesota: Llewellyn Publications, 1990), 205.

4. Gerald B. Gardner, *Witchcraft Today* (Secaucus: New Jersey: Citadel Press, 1973), 18.

5. Paul H. Landis, *Sociology* (Boston: Ginn & Co., 1967), 452.

6. Ibid, 452.

7. Fritz Muntean, "Sacred Names and Mundane Names," *COG Newsletter,* Beltane 1991.

8. Valerie Voigt, "Being Pagan in a 9-to-5 World," *Witchcraft Today Book One: The Modern Craft Movement,* ed. Chas S. Clifton (St. Paul, Minnesota: Llewellyn, 1992).

9. Magenta, "Reply to Sacred Names and Mundane Names," *COG Newsletter,* Beltane 1991.

10. Indeed, Magenta admits that this is probably the bigger problem: that people change their names too often. She is also very adamant that "More important [than what name you use], none of us has the right to make these sort of choices for another. Nobody has the right to decide for another whether or not to reveal mundane names."

11. Sarah Stockwell, "Three Perspectives on the Parliament of the World's Religions," *Tides* 2:1 (Samhain/Yule 1993), 18–19.

12. Darcie, *COG Newsletter,* Lughnasa 1991.

13. Doreen Valiente, ˌ◌◌◌◌◌◌◌◌◌◌◌ ᴃ: ◌2.

14. I started reading about the Craft in 1969, met my first coven in 1974, and was initiated in January 1975.

15. Amber K, 99. Amber is quoting Clifford Bias's *The Ritual Book of Magic.*

16. Lú, "To Know, to Dare, to Will, to Shut Up," *K.A.M., A Journal of Traditional Wicca,* 8.2 (Hallows 1988).

17. Paul Huson, *Mastering Witchcraft: A Practical Guide for Witches, Warlocks, and Covens* (New York, Berkeley, 1970), 30.

18. Lú. He suggests waiting a lunar month before talking about magickal works.

19. Some magicians would argue it's even more important.

20. Dion Fortune, *Applied Magic* (Wellingborough, Northamptonshire: Aquarian, 1976), 12.

21. Ibid, 16.

22. Not her real name, obviously, and not intended to resemble any real person, living or dead.

23. Dennis Coon, *Introduction to Psychology* (St. Paul, Minnesota: West Publishing Co., 1980), 560.

24. Rhianna/WWC, New Age Forum, CompuServe, May 1994.

25. C. C-B, "Out of the Broom Closet with Quiet Dignity and Grace," *Tides,* Samhain/Yule 1993: 35. If you're going to go public, this gives some good tips on how to do it.

26. Not my real name.

About the Author

Although she read her first book on the occult in 1969, it was 1974 before Morven attended her first ritual and 1979 before she attended her first Pagan festival. During the long ride to and from one of those festivals in 1980, Morven co-founded *Harvest* with another area Pagan, Brenwyn. Morven became managing editor in 1982 and produced *Harvest* for twelve years, retiring the publication in 1992.

Since her retirement she has been devoting most of her time to leading a small traditional Alexandrian coven she formed in early 1988. She hopes to see her current round of students graduate in 1995/1996. Though she enjoys celebrating eclectic Pagan and Wiccan rites, and champions the right for anyone to call themselves Pagan and worship the Old Gods, she has a personal goal to restore an updated Alexandrian tradition in her area and train students who can then pass it on to the next generation. In 1995 she celebrated the twentieth anniversary of her initiation into the Alexandrian tradition.

When she is not putting in long hours at her day job, preparing or delivering lessons to her coven, lurking on the Internet, answering the mail that still comes in for *Harvest,* taking care of day-to-day chores, or feeding the birds outdoors, Morven grows magickal herbs and keeps trying to find the time to finish a novel she started in 1978 and a music tape she almost finished in 1984. She lives between the worlds in the MetroWest/Central part of Massachusetts, with her husband, two cats, and three goldfish.

'Tis Evil Luck to Speak of It:

Secrecy and the Craft

By Judy Harrow

Maybe you knew it all your life, knew what you were long before you knew that we have a name. Maybe the trees spoke to you from childhood, as they did to me. Very likely you thought you were the only one. You might even have thought you were crazy, and your parents and teachers may have thought so, too. Then, one day, you somehow discovered that hundreds and thousands of us have similar feelings and experiences—the moment of Homecoming, we call that, the discovery of community. Because we know what alone feels like, community is precious to us.

Even after that, you may have spent a long time looking for the right teacher, the right group, then more time working and studying to prepare for initiation. Finally, they say, you are ready. Whatever was needed, you did it. In a solemn and joyful ritual, you took your vows—Witch and

Priest/ess at last. Initiation may feel to you like the completion of a long process, but the word actually means "beginning." From now on, you get to figure out what Witchcraft is, and what it means to live as a Witch.

Vows of Secrecy

Our many traditions differ in their demands. The precise content of our initiatory vows is, for most of us, an initiatory secret of its own. Still, it is common knowledge that almost all Witches vow ourselves to some form of secrecy. Absolute discretion is our near-universal ideal.

Even the most flatfooted atheist understands that oath-breaking destroys self-esteem. It will also certainly lose us the trust and respect of those who keep their oaths, so oath-breakers exclude themselves from community. For those of us who cherish our relationship with the Gods, the consequences go far beyond even that. If we know what's good for us, we keep faith as best we can!

We keep silence even under torture, right? Here's bedrock truth: nobody knows. In the Burning Times, we are told, it was easy to know what one should do but desperately hard to do it. In some places in this world, there still are knocks on the door in the dead of the night. All anybody can know is how they hope they will conduct themselves at such a time. Nobody knows for sure how they will act in extremity, and the wise pray never to find out. Realistically, and thankfully, we in the English-speaking world are most unlikely to face such stark horror.

Our challenge, instead, is discerning what we should do. Instead of brutal force, many of us will confront ambiguity and confusion, a gray and foggy path with few guiding landmarks. Other needs and values may come into conflict with our traditions of silence. Know this: as you sit reading this essay, some Witch, somewhere, is struggling with a difficult decision about whether, who, and how much to tell. Imagine what that feels like. This is the crisis you will likely face some day.

Are all these oaths we take just hypocrisy? Should we cop to it and stop the practice—just trust our own best Witchy instincts to guide us through the complexities and let it go at that?

At least one of my students sees it that way. He figures that his own students know right from wrong. During their training, he makes sure they have plenty of chance to think through and talk through the issues that they are likely to encounter, so they can be as mentally and emotionally prepared as possible. By the time that he is willing to elevate them, he feels that he had better be willing to trust them, without oathing, without binding. The good training he gives them should be sufficient.

I agree that thought experiments and behavioral rehearsals are both necessary and extremely valuable. If not, it would be stupid to write about these issues. However, even our best thought alone is not sufficient. Human behavior springs more from the heart and the gut than from the head. As priest/esses, we understand that careful forethought works best when reinforced by ritual, which speaks to the younger and deeper self. An oath is a voluntarily accepted, cooperatively worked binding spell.

We make some very basic choices about how we want to act—really about who we want to be. Then, by vowing ourselves to them, we instill these decisions firmly and deeply into ourselves, creating an anchor to our own core values. If this work of binding is well and truly done, we will not casually or carelessly violate our standards, or compromise our values for convenience or gain. I would expect the oaths I have taken to protect me from panic and to strengthen me in times of critical stress.

However, I do not at all expect my oaths, simple statements made for and by the inner child, to help me sort through the complexities, the conflicts, the many shades of gray. This is the task of the inner adult. My oaths help me live by my decisions; they do not help me decide. Instead, we can help each other by thinking together about these issues. Ritual, too, is necessary but not sufficient.

Since none of us has perfect knowledge or perfect wisdom, all we can do when we face complex and ambiguous choices is to act as seems best, take responsibility for whatever we do, and be willing to learn hard lessons from our own mistakes. Believe me, those mistakes can be public and painful. Therefore, I offer, as at least a starting point, what I have learned in the seventeen years since my own initiation.

First, let's define some issues involving secrecy. Secrecy about people, their concerns, and their involvement with Witchcraft is different from secrecy about our stories, symbols, rituals, and magical techniques. There is also a difference, known since classical times but rarely articulated, between the kinds of secrets that can, but should not, be told, and the mysteries, which are deeply internal, experiential, and non-verbal. There are very different issues, with very different possible consequences to be considered for each of these.

Beyond even that, the Wiccan Rede, "An [If] it harm none, do what ye will," is our core ethic, by which whatever else we may do—including our vows—is informed, guided, evaluated and, if need be, set aside. In those few

and terrible moments when the Rede and our vows conflict, we truly face the abyss. May Ancient Wisdom guide
us then.

Personal Confidentiality: the Secrecy of Who We Are

The violation of a person's privacy has never been and is
still not tolerated in our community. While many things
have changed since Gerald Gardner's time, this is a constant: those who violate others' privacy or even threaten to
do so, will almost certainly find themselves ostracized as
oath-breakers.

Every Witch or Pagan has the absolute right to decide
for themselves who shall know how much about their religious affiliation. The way to know how public a Witch is
willing to be is simply to ask them. In very rare circumstances where you are truly not able to ask them, follow
their example. Be careful not to rely on old statements or
behaviors. The right to choose implies the right to change
one's mind. Perhaps she was open in the freewheeling
atmosphere of a college town, but now she is struggling to
establish a professional career. Perhaps he is in a new relationship, and his new lover has a stronger sense of privacy
than the last one. Saying that somebody who had their legal
name in the letters column of some obscure publication
twenty years ago has yielded all right to privacy is about
like saying that only virgins can ever say no.

Each of us is the world's greatest authority on our own
life and needs. Each person's situation is different. Some traditions specifically require that their members maintain
personal secrecy. Many other Witches feel that, by publicly
identifying themselves as Witches, they would risk their
jobs, their homes, even the custody of their children. At

times, in places, this fear is still accurate. Whether or not it is, each of us chooses our own level of risk. The rest of us do not get to second guess.

People make a wide variety of choices. Some keep their faith entirely to themselves. Others appear on television talk shows for all to see. Some are out to their friends, but not at work. Some people want to reserve their legal name for their professional lives, and use some other chosen name within the Pagan community. Others want their Craft names used only in circle, preferring to use their legal name in ordinary space. We respect others' choices and expect their respect for our own.

Once out of the broom closet, voluntarily or otherwise, a person can never entirely go back (although that's no excuse for further outing). To "out" a person against their own will is to deprive them of that choice forever, to do them irreparable harm. Whether or not any secondary harm comes of it, they are subjected to the psychological stress of risks they did not choose and perhaps were not ready to take. It's not "just" the initiatory oath that has been broken—it is the Rede!

You may think that a friend is being overly timid. You may think they are exaggerating the dangers of their situation. If this is your opinion, and if they are willing to hear it, then, certainly, you may try to persuade them. The following are some of the arguments for openness.

We aren't nearly as hidden as some of us fondly believe we are. We may actually be making it difficult for sincere seekers to find their way Home, while any determined researcher could dig up telephone and computer e-mail records, perhaps even the subscription lists of magazines or records of who attended gatherings. How about credit card or even mail-order purchases of Wicca-related books?

Where we really stand is halfway out of the broom closet, and that's the point of greatest danger: subject to trial and condemnation by rumor, not yet fully protected by legal and customary standards of freedom of religion. The only way to win our full freedom is to come out—not every single one of us, but those who feel they can, and enough of us to make an impact.

If we do not define ourselves, others will define us. By our silence we cede to them the power of naming. Nor are the outsiders who would define us always our friends. They are not always objective. They are not even always honest. We have more to worry about these days than stupid cartoon movies that nobody takes seriously anyhow. Some extremist fundamentalist writers are actively pushing the old lies about devil worship and human sacrifice. The perpetrators of the ritual-abuse panic have victims with hypnotically induced pseudo-memories who can and do act as convincing "witnesses." By our robes, candles and pentagrams, we are vulnerable to these lies.

Living in hiding, nurturing a secret, is also psychologically toxic. We can come to believe that we are special, heroic, armchair martyrs. The alienation and paranoia that this breeds eventually becomes a self-fulfilling prophecy, as our furtive behavior draws response in kind from those around us. People who know us personally—family, friends, co-workers—can often sense that we are withholding something from them. If they feel we're hiding something, it's easier for them to believe that we have something unwholesome to hide.

Staying in touch, and being open, with people of other religions and of none provides us with a healthy reality check. Access to a trusted outside perspective can help us avoid some of the flakier theories and practices that sometimes slop over from the fringes of the magical or New Age communities, or to recognize when some leader is abusing his or her role or some group has become dysfunctional. Yes, these things can happen anywhere. The more isolated the community or group, the more intellectually stagnant, the more likely delusion or abuse becomes.

Most important, I think, is the issue of walking our talk. We say we are an Earth religion, finding our ultimate meaning and value in this life on this Earth here and now. Strict separation of secular and religious life seems to me to be inconsistent with geocentric thealogy. If we are called, as I believe we are, to protect, serve and heal Mother Earth in this time of crisis—well, I just do not see how we can effectively do that from a closet!

For these reasons, I am very "out." I am writing this under my legal name. I have done media work, using my legal name, for years, and I frequently and publicly encourage everybody to be as out as they possibly can, to actually "push the envelope" on openness. Here is a surprise: in all these years, I have never heard a word of criticism from those Witches who adhere to older traditions of personal secrecy. They respect my choices as long as I am willing to respect and protect theirs. Though our choices differ, we share a commitment to choice itself.

The core issue is mutual respect, not secrecy; it is the trust that we must have to re-create our community. Those who are most private need to know in their guts that even the media Witches will protect them. Otherwise they can and will protect themselves by avoiding interaction, hiding from the rest of us as they do from the cowan. This is the universal basic, and absolutely necessary social contract" among us. Because we know what alone feels like, community is precious to us, and we will protect it. Your continued participation in the Wiccan/Pagan community in large part depends upon your keeping this trust.

Craft Secrecy and Secular Law

Very early one morning in the gray Northeast, a Witch was murdered in her own home. The police, who found no sign of forced entry, concluded that the killer must have been someone she knew well enough to open the door for them in the pre-dawn hours. Since the dead woman had been active in a local Pagan organization, they requested a copy of the group's membership roster.

Few questions are purely legal. Consider this: the close friends and colleagues of the murdered woman very much wanted to cooperate with the investigation in any way they could. They did not want the local media to get the impression that the Witches were obstructing a murder investigation. However, the legal issue here was stark. The police request could easily have been followed by a subpoena. Refusing such a subpoena would have been followed by jail time for contempt of court. Thankfully, because they had been out in their community for many years and were well known, the Witches were able to persuade the district attorney to withdraw the request.

We'd like to think that as priest/esses, as clergy, our communications with coven members are legally protected, "privileged" communication. We would like to believe that our religious status safeguards us, at least, from the threat of jail, but it is not that simple.

In 1994, members of a Florida Wiccan group were accused of zoning violations—of operating a church in a residential area—because they had a Maypole in their backyard at Beltane. They fought and won their case on the local level, but they had to take a second mortgage on their house to pay their lawyer as they carry on a federal lawsuit to establish a stronger precedent that will protect others as well. Not all of us are homeowners. What legal rights we have are only made real when we have the resources and the determination to defend them.

In addition, the legal right of any clergy to remain silent varies from state to state and with the type of case. Many states, for example, mandate the reporting of child abuse. Ten years ago, also in Florida, a fundamentalist Christian minister, the Rev. John Mellish, counseled a child abuser in his congregation and actually persuaded the man to surrender himself to the authorities. The man confessed, pled guilty, and still the court demanded the pastor's testimony. Pastor Mellish refused on principle and went to jail for contempt of court, setting an honorable example for all clergy of all religions. Understand that where the law denies the privilege of confidential communication to anybody, a Witch cannot claim religious discrimination.

Each of us needs to research what the law actually is where we live, in order to assess our risks and protect ourselves as best we can. No protection is perfect, and some apparent protections do more harm than good.

At the height of the ritual-abuse scare, some members of one major Wiccan group proposed a policy statement dissociating the group from any illegal activities on the part of any of its members. This was called the "cover your anatomy amendment." It was never adopted because the law of the land does not—and should not—control our consciences.

In fact, we do condone some illegal activities. Sometimes a person's spirituality and conscience call them to break the law—trespassing and blockading to defend ancient forests, for example. In some places, activities directly related to our religion, such as reading the Tarot, are illegal. Better to keep quiet than to say we condone some illegal activities but not others.

Therefore, we keep quiet whenever possible. We stay as far away from cowan courts and cowan cops as we possibly can. This is traditional advice and good advice but not an absolute. The Rede from which our religion grows tells us that the only absolute is to avoid harm. This is the hard part: sometimes to avoid harm, by the Rede itself, we must break silence.

My secular profession, counseling, has its own strong tradition of confidentiality. Professional counselors, however, acknowledge clear limits to that confidentiality, and good reasons for those limits. Witches can learn from this example. In the early 1970s, Tatiana Tarasoff was a student at the University of California. Another student, obsessed with thoughts of murdering her, sought help at the university counseling center. His counselor, a licensed psychologist, kept his confidence and did not warn Tatiana. She was murdered. Her parents won a wrongful death suit. The California Supreme Court upheld the decision on appeal (Tarasoff v. Regents of the University of California, 1976) and so established a legal "duty to warn" in situations of serious danger to self or others.

Jail is not a good enough reason to break silence, but, by the Rede, saving a life is.

Sometimes, as with Tarasoff, the danger is individual and specific. Sometimes it is more general. One of the great heroes of my generation is the whistleblower Daniel Ellsberg, who saved many lives by illegally releasing classified material to the press, material that exposed the massive falsehoods that were used to rationalize the American invasion of Vietnam. Ellsberg predictably lost a job that paid very well and carried a great deal of prestige and power. His former colleagues doubtlessly saw him as a traitor. He risked jail. A generation earlier, he might have risked execution.

At a Pagan gathering in upstate New York, we had a case of stupid crudeness. The guy was repeatedly and annoyingly hitting on women, he had wandering hands, and he did not stop when clearly told to do so. Sexual harassment, no doubt about it, but nowhere near rape. We called together a council of responsible elders, decided what to do, and informed the man that he was not welcome back next year, or any other year until we heard from his local community that he had learned to treat women with respect. A distasteful situation, but one that posed no immediate or serious danger, quietly handled within the community.

Meanwhile, further west, other Witches faced a similar case of stupid crudeness at local open circles. Here, too, the women were annoyed, but they were not injured or endangered. They could have simply declared the guy *persona non grata*. Instead they brought criminal charges. The over-reaction and its backlash tore their community apart.

Here's a guide: we can trust the Gods for retributive justice. Our responsibility is prevention and healing only. We should settle problems internally whenever we can. We must never break silence for trivial or ulterior reasons.

However, sometimes the fire fighters gets to see the inside of the temple. Some situations carry imminent and serious danger that truly is beyond our ability to handle within the community.

We may break silence only when we must—only when, as for Daniel Ellsberg, the potential consequences to self or others of keeping silence outweigh the full consequences of breaking it.

Until and unless you are prepared to look the Crone in the eye, tell Her, "Yes, I broke my oath, and here's why," and accept Her judgement, don't do it. Perhaps She will agree with you, but you have no guarantee. Don't you ever dare try to second guess Her. May we all stay aware of what conscientious whistleblowers put on the line, and may this awareness keep us honest!

Criminal law concerns itself with behavior that the whole community considers wrongful and damaging to the collective. On the other side of the courthouse, civil law is about resolving disputes between individuals. Civil disputes almost never involve imminent serious danger.

The Ardanes say "'Tis the old Law and the most important of all Laws that no one may do anything which will endanger any of the Craft, or bring them into contact with the law of the land....In any disputes between the brethren, no one may invoke any laws but those of the Craft or any tribunal but that of the Priestess, Priest, and Elders. And may the Curse of the Goddess be on any who do so."[1]

That reads like an absolute prohibition, and it is. Even so, we all know Witches who have sued other Witches in court without being ostracized for it, most commonly if they are getting a legal divorce. In realistic terms, the prohibition is against bringing Witchcraft, not individual Witches, before the bench.

There are two main reasons to discourage lawsuits among Witches. One is that disputes over actual Wiccan issues are not under any circumstance to be taken into secular courts—the cowans do not get a vote in our business. Secondly, even when the issue to be settled is entirely secular, you must not "out" each other as Witches in court. Revealing that the opponent is a Witch might be "good tactics." It might help you win your case, might even win you a lot of money. However, by taking that advantage you reinforce the notion that there's something weird or wrong about being a Witch, reason enough to decide against one of us.

It's happened. A Witch once sued a Wiccan organization because another Witch had left an inheritance to it and not to her. Another Witch threatened both to sue and to publicly name "and not just their Craft names" other Witches who had gotten in the way of some of his political plans. I recently heard another Witch threaten to sue some Witches because their protests about his sloppy confidentiality spoiled a business deal of his. It happens. It's ugly. The feedback is usually both swift and dramatic.

Therefore, I offer another guideline. You might find yourself suing or being sued by another Witch. This is an

unfortunate and a delicate situation. Even as you argue out
your differences in that very adversarial setting, you must
somehow cooperate in keeping the silence; whichever side
mentions Witchcraft first has broken trust.

The Mysteries: Soul Secrets

We are nature mystics. We are magic users. Neat phrases,
but they mean almost nothing unless you have been there
and done that. Magic and mysticism are to be lived, not
described. They are, in essence, nonverbal.

At one phase of my life I collected and read a lot of cookbooks. Reading cookbooks is not at all the same activity as
cooking. Cooking is about smell, texture, taste—a sensuous
experience that cannot be reduced to words. It is the same
with sewing, carpentry, sex, ice skating, and what Witches
do in circle.

As nature mystics, we work with altered states of consciousness, with ecstasy. We listen together for the sacred
voices on the wind. We look together for the sacred faces in
the stones. We chant and dance and dream together.
Through all this and more, we seek to deepen our conscious contact with the Immanent Divine, Who we experience as Mother Earth. We feel Her power in us. We feel
ourselves part of Her body.

Some will hear that as simple truth, some as metaphor,
and still others as nonsense. The greater mysteries cannot
be told to those unready to hear. People have understood
this since ancient times—the details of the Eleusinian rituals were strictly protected by law, but the core meaning
never was.

You can tell other people of the mysteries, if you like,
without community censure, but you do so at your own

risk. Those who are not ready to hear may think you are weird, irrational, unreliable, even delusional. A reputation like that could hurt you on the job. If you persist, they may think you are a fanatic, a bore, maybe even a Satanist. That's why tradition advises us to let ourselves be judged more by our deeds than our words.

However, although unwise or premature revelations may hurt you, they will do no damage to the mysteries. Remember, these are mysteries, not secrets. People will screen out whatever they are not ready to hear. Whoever does hear is ready, Witch or not. There is no downside to enlightenment. The Goddess is nobody's private property; She is Mother to all that lives.

We are in conscious contact with Her only imperfectly and intermittently. We are obstructed by old hurts and old habits. We try together to open our own channel to the Sacred, to clear the blockages. Mysticism shades into magic when we work towards our own psychospiritual healing and growth.

Magic has been defined as "the art of changing consciousness in accordance with will." Changes we make inside ourselves often create secondary results in our interactions with others. When consciousness changes, behavior changes, and different behavior calls forth different responses. To change my consciousness is to change my life in all aspects, not just the religious. Healing magic, love magic, job magic—all grow from this root.

Although the greater mysteries themselves require no secrecy, this delicate inner work most certainly does. In the quiet intimacy of our small circles, we minister to each other. All are clergy; all are congregants. Each of us brings to the circle our deepest needs, our most painful inner wounds and scars, our newest and most fragile inner growth. Together, we create the context for one another's psychospiritual development. For this, we must have utterly safe space. Few would risk exposing themselves this deeply if their struggles are likely to become common gossip. Therefore, whatever is said and done within a cast circle is not normally to be discussed with anyone who was not present, not even other Witches.

Human growth takes place both through a gradual and constant process, and through a few dramatic moments of radical personal transformation—initiations. Sometimes we are suddenly changed by something that happens in the normal course of life, such as having a baby. Other initiations are carefully structured rituals, something that our elders do to and for us.

Witchcraft is one such initiatory path. Initiations and elevations are our greatest acts of magic. They work by separating us from ordinary contexts and mind-sets, disorienting us, carrying us to the liminal state, the threshold of change. A candidate for initiation must let go completely, trust him- or herself utterly to the elder or initiator.

Effective initiation requires surprise. If candidates hear verbal descriptions in advance, they will form expectations. Humans are very good at seeing what we expect to see, rather than what is there. If the candidate's perceptual abilities are trammeled by expectations, they will force their experience into that mold. They will miss some part, perhaps the heart, of what is presented to them.

Only the silence of all prior initiates can guarantee initiatory surprise. If you talk to non-initiates about what happens at initiations, you risk spoiling their experience and compromising our future.

Craft Secrets: The Technology of the Sacred

Remember *Fantasia,* the classic Disney film? Mickey Mouse plays the sorcerer's apprentice, assigned by his master to fetch water. Instead, as soon as the old man's back is turned, Mickey peeks into a forbidden grimoire and finds a spell for turning the broom into a robot that carries the heavy pails up the long staircase. Great, but there's just one problem. Mickey never thought to find a spell to make the robot stop. By the time the sorcerer returns, the place is flooded, and Mickey is in big trouble.

We say, "If that grimoire were available, there'd be a whole lot of wet floors around here." We also say, "There's nothing immoral about a bread knife, but I sure wouldn't hand one to my two-year-old." We guard our knowledge as if it were a dangerous thing, and, as all power is danger, it is.

No, I do not know how to make brooms carry water, but I do know how to change consciousness in accordance with will, in lots of ways. The Witch's Craft is the technology of the sacred, a set of methods for making ecstasy happen. We learn and practice them as a pianist practices scales, for what they will enable us to do. These techniques and skills, directed toward psychospiritual change, support both mysticism and magic.

Like any powerful technology, our Craft can help or harm. Like any technology, it needs to be handled with caution, wisdom, restraint, and care. Our basic sense of responsibility demands that we wisely share what we know. It could be temptingly easy, especially for beginners suddenly finding themselves with such powerful techniques, to use them for self-aggrandizement, or to intervene without permission in the lives of others "for their own good."

Therefore, by tradition, we teach our students one-on-one or in very small groups where we can get to know each one well. This allows us to monitor their personal development, making very sure that they understand traditional ethics and cautions. In an organic teaching process, we carefully transfer only those skills that we feel they are ready for, that they can use wisely and well.

Indeed, some traditions ask their newly elevated elders to wait a while, until what they've learned is tempered by experience, before taking on students of their own. Some real life experience will help them make the judgment calls about pacing instruction. Far from being authoritarian or overly restrictive, this is classic "student-centered education."

We guard our techniques for the very best of reasons— or do we? We need to look to our own motivations. This could all be a rationalization for hanging on to some real or imagined monopoly. You will see it blatantly stated as the reason for secrecy in some of the older occult books: "power shared is power lost." Maybe, if you seek and wield the abusive power of the dominator. In a partnership model, knowledge shared is knowledge multiplied.

If I know something that my neighbor does not know, even if my neighbor is fully capable of learning it, I could get to feeling special, superior to my neighbor. I might even begin to convince myself that I am entitled to use what I know to push my neighbor around. In short, keeping our techniques to ourselves could tempt us into exactly those misbehaviors that we thought we were preventing.

Wiccan tradition offers us a common-sense resolution: "Let the Craft keep books with the names of all herbs which are good for people, and all cures, so all may learn. But keep another book with all the Bales and Apies [poisons and opiates] and let only the Elders and other trustworthy people have this knowledge."[2]

A large part of the Ardanes is about how to keep a secret under persecution. In contrast with all that, this passage is startling. We are told to share healing knowledge widely, even at the risk of self-exposure (everybody in the village would know that this old lady is good with herbs). However, some life-saving herbs, such as foxglove, are also dangerous. Only those with considerable skill should handle them. Therefore, that part of the information is restricted to to elders and "trustworthy people." Notice that nothing is said about whether these trustworthy folk are "of the brethren" or not.

To be honest, we do also have a few "secrets" that are fairly trivial, on the order of "secret club handshakes" that allow us to know our own. Any healthy community needs some sense of secure boundaries. We do not harm anybody by withholding our little in-jokes and passwords.

Whatever will help people to heal and grow, that we should share with anyone of good heart who is curious. The techniques that we know are not really ours. There are no secrets except those of Mother Nature, and She is a blabbermouth. We are under obligation to conserve this knowledge, develop it, and share it with "trustworthy people" of any path.

Synergistic Knowledge: Is Now the Time to Share?

Pagan religious movements, dormant in European and European-derived culture for fifteen hundred years, are now resurgent. What has changed? What allows this rebirth?

When patriarchal monotheism gained ascendancy, we lost access to the culture's means of communication. In isolated pockets, stagnant, our knowledge atrophied. In this century, however, communication has become faster, easier and, most important, decentralized. We rewove our web by little newsletters, by long drives, by massive phone bills, and most recently by enthusiastic use of computer nets. Witches, traditional holders of mystical secrets, are also avid communicators.

In this time of Neopagan renascence, those of us who are committed to making it happen have a double task before us. One is to recreate the culture, the skills, the knowledge base that was destroyed and lost over the centuries. The other is to teach the young all we know in a way that leaves them free to discover more. Only thus, by not falling back into stagnation, can we honor our predecessors, who created a foundation for us out of almost nothing.

Right now, the need is too great for us to hide what we know from each other. When we share our discoveries, we avoid wasteful duplication of work. Others can help us avoid pitfalls they already found the hard way, or they might spot connections or opportunities we would have missed. Working collaboratively maximizes each person's effectiveness. Yes, we need to be careful who we teach how to change human consciousness, but we also need to weigh the risks of overcautiousness. We need to find our balance.

Go back to the old stories. Too many restrictions, followed too scrupulously, can kill the spirit. Cuchulainn, forbidden to eat the flesh of dogs and equally forbidden to refuse hospitality, was undone when he was offered dog meat for dinner, a classic double bind.

More often than not, it is easy to know what to do. Our traditions give us good guidance, and other wisdom, human and Divine, can be available to us. Sometimes, however, it is very hard. Sometimes we are confronted with difficult, or even tragic, choices. The obligations of silence, the needs of communication, these can pull us apart. They can undo us as Cuchulainn's conflicting geasa undid him.

They need not. Remember the stories of the third path. Between the straight, narrow road to heaven and the broad, flowery way to hell lies the almost invisible, winding track to Fairyland.

We draw power from polarity, and this is yet another point of balance. We can hold silence and communication in dynamic tension, making careful choices in each new situation, taking responsibility and always, always learning. We can act as Witches. We can grow.

Notes

1. Lady Sheba, *The Book of Shadows* (St. Paul, Minnesota: Llewellyn Publications, 1971), Ardanes #127–129. The "Ardanes" (a variant spelling of "ordains") are the basic code of conduct of English Traditional Witchcraft.

2. Ibid, #136–137.

About the Author

Judy Harrow is high priestess of Proteus Coven in New York City, and currently serving as public information officer of Covenant of the Goddess. She also holds a master's degree in counseling. Her previous contributions to the

Witchcraft Today series were "Other People's Kids: Working with the Underaged Seeker" and "Initiation by Ordeal: Military Service as a Passage to Adulthood," both published in Book Two *Modern Rites of Passage*

She wishes to thank her colleagues in the Greywoods Study Group and other Witches who will recognize themselves for interactions that helped her think more clearly about these issues.

The Us-Them Dichotomy

by Malcolm Brenner

It had been an almost perfect day. Seafoam and I had spent it touring Washington's Olympic Peninsula in the company of another Pagan couple, Titania and Haricot.[1] Cruising the open roads in their car, we had enjoyed beautiful fall scenery, good food, and stimulating conversation. A deep sense of commonality had emerged, and with it the tacit knowledge that magic was once again afoot.

That night, riding the ferry across Puget Sound to Seattle, we marveled at the brilliant auroras playing overhead. The darkness was redolent with mysteries profound. I remarked on the beauty of Nature, and how, as Witches, we were in a special position to appreciate it.

"Yes," said Titania. "Aren't we lucky the Gods chose us?"

Seafoam and I exchanged a long, slow look.

"Pardon me," I said, "but what did you just say?"

"Why, how lucky we are that the Gods chose us to be Witches and worship them," Titania said, smiling benignly.

"Yes, we count ourselves fortunate to be among the Chosen Ones," Haricot said, his voice capitalizing the words. "Surely, you feel the same way too—don't you?"

Now, Seafoam and I did not agree on everything; some days, it seemed like we did not agree on anything. However, one thing we agreed upon—we had been talking about it just the day before—was that this notion that some people are "chosen by God" (or "the Gods") was one of the most delusional, pernicious, and potentially dangerous fallacies to which the human mind can fall victim.

"Why, no," I said slowly, feeling a chill in the blustery breeze. "We choose the Gods! Seafoam and I are quite clear about that."

"Oh? How's that?" Titania asked, uncertain.

"It goes like this," I said. "If you believe you are, for some reason, 'chosen' by a divinity, then you have that divinity's stamp of approval. Ergo, no matter what you do, you can do no wrong, because it's sanctioned by God. That's fundamentalism."

Titania and Haricot stared at us, startled.

"That self-justifying attitude has led to some of the most hideous atrocities in human history, including, need I add, the Burning Times," Seafoam added.

"If we believe we choose the Gods, it makes us responsible for our belief systems and our behavior, not the other way around," I said.

Titania sighed, turned, and walked into the ferry's lounge. After a second, Haricot followed.

"Gee, do you think we said something wrong?" Seafoam asked.

The drive back to our apartment was made in uncomfortable silence. They bid us a terse good night and split, the sense of commonality we had enjoyed all day having been displaced by distance and distrust.

That was the beginning of a number of disagreements that rent the Seattle Pagan community for the better part of a decade, and continue in some form to this day. Ever since, I have been haunted by the question "What makes us Witches?"

The question is one of communication. The most basic distinction we can make, the one that is made for us at birth, is between the self and other—the "me/you" dichotomy. Although it gets blurred in events such as eating, sex, and pregnancy, the physical distinction is usually pretty obvious: where I stop, you may begin. If we lose track of the mental boundaries between ourselves and others, we may fall victim to mental illnesses ranging from mild neuroses (cold mom makes warm kid wear sweater) to full-blown psychoses (Is that You talking to me, Jehovah?).

However, there is another dimension to this question of self and other. In phylogenetic terms, as soon as we rise from amoebas to slime-molds, we run into the phenomena of creatures who form themselves into groups, like hives of insects, schools of fish, flocks of birds, or herds of mammals. The group is a more stable formation than the individual. It can perform feats the individual cannot, such as enhancing reproduction and food-gathering activities and thwarting predation. For many animals, inclusion or exclusion from the group spells the difference between life and death.

Typically, we humans carry this in-group/out-group identification to absurd lengths. When animals support others who share their genes, ethologist Edmund O. Wilson dubs it "sociobiology." Would it be fair to say that humans have turned this around and invented "biosociology"—the imitation of natural selection among competing human belief systems?

Rather than shared genes, we often define group membership by things as subtle as skin pigmentation, hair style, ornaments, accent, or make of car. For instance, among the Dineh (Navajos), one very important in-group defining factor, after clan relations, is mastery of the difficult language. As a reporter living and working among the Dineh, even very feeble attempts on my part to learn the language were met with greater acceptance, not to mention considerable amusement.

The ultimate in-group discriminators are based on intangibles such as, most potently, belief systems. Belief systems (or "cognitive rules" in sociological terms) are potent in-group/out-group definers precisely because they don't necessarily manifest outwardly. Hidden, they require elucidation. As J. Douglas and F. Waksler explain in *The Sociology of Deviance,* "Violations of basic rules of cognition are generally believed by members of groups to be socially threatening. Extreme cognitive deviance may even be viewed as threatening to all social order or as leading to universal chaos."[2] Also, because they deal with software and not hardware, belief systems can be changed, affecting every aspect of an individual's existence. In defining human groups, they transcend biology and genetics.

"In 1959 I met a lovely man of White Mountain Apache descent," writes Sandra Bickham, a member of the Church of All Worlds.[3] "After a courtship of six months, we decided to marry." Because her fiancée was a member of the American Indian Council, representatives of ten tribes were present at their wedding in Washington.

"As I stood in the back of the church, as nervous as any bride has ever been, one of the Elders came to speak to me. He informed me that they could not allow me to marry Eddie because I was not Indian," Bickham writes. "I was terrified. I loved Eddie and wanted to marry him, but I also respected the Elders."

The elder then solved the problem he had raised by suggesting that Bickham allow herself to be "adopted" by one of the tribes. This was her dream come true. "All my life I had decried the fates that caused me to be born Caucasian," she writes. "I have/had very little respect for the race I was born into. I had always wished I could have been born American Indian, or Asian." An impromptu "adoption" ceremony was held in the back of the church, Bickham became a member of what she calls the "White Sands Navajo Tribe,"[4] and the wedding proceeded. The ceremony of adoption had served to change her racial identity for herself and the people to whom it mattered.

Personally, I find Bickham's attitude toward her racial identity sad. As Wiccans we should come to terms with our roots and realize we, too, were an oppressed people. We should not be ashamed of our European ancestry, only of our behavior as imperialists and colonizers—behaviors also found among Amerindians and Asians. We should not romanticize them. As Witches, we are in a long line of victims of such in-group/out-group discriminations, along with African-Americans, Native Americans, and Sino-Soviet peasants. We can hide our pentagrams, but we cannot for the most part hide the distinctive attitudes and values that set us apart from the rest of modern Western society. Often, it is simply our inherent "Witchiness" that betrays us.

Let me give an example from my personal experience.

Seafoam and I lived in an apartment complex in Port-land, Oregon, in the late 1980s. So many managers came and went through this place that their apartment should have had a revolving door on it. The good managers, concerned with the welfare of the tenants and the build-ings, never stayed long, while the mediocre ones tended to endure. Most just left us alone as long as we paid the rent on time. However, the last managers we dealt with were members of a small, militantly Jehovan[5] church in the neighborhood.

For almost all of the time we lived there, an ornament given us by one of our Craft friends hung in our window, a crescent moon inside the symbol for "female." A couple of our neighbors asked us about it, but most people ignored it, and a few admired it. It was not anything bla-tant like a pentagram.

One dark Moon night I was going to put a binding spell on a local business that had not paid me for a photographic job. It was nothing much; I just planned to carry a candle around the place three times clockwise while muttering the appropriate incantations, which I made up on the spot and have since forgotten. Since the business was on a main road I eschewed my robes in favor of a common windbreaker—alas, white.

As I was leaving the apartment complex, a stray black cat approached me, begging attention and probably food. Thinking this a favorable omen I spent a few minutes play-ing with the cat. At the time I remember looking up at the lighted window of the managers' apartment and wondering what they would make of this if they could see me. Then, giving the cat directions to my apartment if it wanted a caring home, I went about my task.

I found out exactly what the managers had been thinking a couple of weeks later when they gave us a thirty-day eviction notice, thus avoiding having to give us a reason for the eviction under Oregon law. Friends whom the managers trusted passed on this choice bit of gossip: they had interpreted the symbol in our window as "occult," although, since they were undoubtedly fearful of confronting us arch-fiends face-to-face, they never asked us about it. Seeing me wandering around after sundown, they had taken out binoculars to watch me playing with the cat, and that had been too much for them. Seafoam and I were branded as Satanists. (Come to think of it, Seafoam's half-brother having an attack of Tourette's Syndrome in the parking lot probably didn't help either.)

Yes, the spell worked; the business compensated me. The cat moved in and proved to be a monster from Hell, nearly taking out our six-year-old daughter's eye. We staved off the eviction as long as we could; we even considered fighting it in court on religious discrimination grounds, but were advised we did not stand much chance. Under Oregon law, the eviction was legal.

Now I know why Witches wear black. Never mind Laurie Cabot's explanations; it's just harder to see at night!

I could give other examples from my own history and that of others—the infamous incidents involving the Grove of the Unicorn in Athens, Georgia, come to mind—but almost every Witch has a couple of similar stories. This is the type of persecution we face on a daily basis—invidious, pernicious, malicious, and often perfectly legal. While we are not presently being burned at the stake in the U.S.A., we are still widely reviled, misunderstood, castigated, and discriminated against in the work place, the media and the courts—and among our own kind.

When I wanted to place some of the earlier books in this series in a Pagan-organized crafts fair recently, I was told I would have to take a booth in the back of the hall. The books had "Witchcraft" in the title, "and we don't want to frighten off the blue-haired little old ladies," an organizer said. Needless to say I declined his generous offer, with imprecations.

Removing our societal status as a discriminated out-group will tend to lessen our persecution, reduce our stress levels, and increase Wicca's chances of being accepted as a valid spiritual tradition—aw, heck, as a religion, then. Therefore, understanding what I call "the us-them dichotomy"—how we (in-group, Pagans), and they (out-group, non-Pagans) differently perceive us; the reasons for these perceptions; and their effects—is of vital importance not only to us as individual Witches but to the acceptance and survival of the Craft at large.

My question, "What makes us Witches?" breaks down into an inner and an outer part. First, and most important, how do we define ourselves and recognize each other as "of the Craft," to be pleasantly archaic? To put it in academic jargon, what are the consensual in-group boundaries of the personal belief paradigm of Wicca?

In the first example, Seafoam and I had never seriously considered that a Witch could honestly feel "chosen by the Gods" in the same way a televangelist says he feels "chosen by Christ." As we analyzed our individual paths to the Craft, we found we were always afforded sets of choices that led either toward or away from Wicca. The steps we had taken were not always consciously in the direction of Wicca, particularly early in our lives, but the appearance of free will to decide yes or no, left or right, had always been there. Encountering what appeared to be an opposite belief system in Titania and Haricot made us doubt their intentions. We still recognized them as fellow Witches because of their belief in the Goddess and their rituals, but not the sort of Witches with whom we wanted to become involved.

Let me give you another example. A year or so after that incident, a group of people calling themselves Witches moved into town and set up shop selling ceremonial tools and copies of what they claimed to be an "authentic" seventeenth-century grimoire. After visiting their covenstead and encountering attitudes of persecution and paranoia, not to mention a room full of high-caliber weaponry, Seafoam and I decided not to mess with them or their fake grimoires.

Sometime later we received a call from Shadowhawk, one of our teachers and an acknowledged elder in the Seattle Craft community. A woman and children from the group had come to her with injuries and stories of physical, emotional, sexual, and ritual abuse. After discussion, a consensus was reached among the community elders that this coven was flaunting the Wiccan Rede, "An ye harm none, do what you will." If they were not following the Wiccan Rede, they were not Witches; ergo, they were not entitled to protection under our oaths of confidentiality. Child Protective Services was notified of the abuse. The woman and her children went to a shelter. It was found that two members of the group were wanted for questioning in connection with a death in another country. They were deported, and I don't know what happened to them.

In this case, the boundaries of the belief paradigm of Wicca were clearly violated and just as clearly reinforced by appropriate community action. Simply put, none of us were willing to put up with that kind of bullshit from people calling themselves "Witches," and if they were going to pull that kind of bullshit we weren't going to let them call themselves "Witches" in our neck of the woods.

Such clear-cut cases of community consent are, unfortunately, the exception rather than the rule. Because we (thank Goddess!) lack the dogma or "revealed works" of other religions, gray areas constantly arise in the definition of "Witch," both within our community and outside it.

Some members of traditions such as Gardnerian and Alexandrian are reluctant to recognize the self-initiate as a legitimate Witch, since she or he has not been through formal training, or received orthodox initiation in rituals that involve lots of kissing of daggers and so on. I know of a coven that denies membership based on race: "Your guardian angel is African and we practice only Celtic mysteries. Go find yourself a Santería priest." Others base it on gender: "Only women can really be Witches!"—thus reinforcing a sexist stereotype. (Bad enough that so many people still think a male Witch is called a "warlock," when that term actually meant "one who narcs on Witches.") Still others base recognition on compliance with authority. One coven's Book of Shadows states, "If the High Priest says 'Jump!' it is permitted of the initiate to ask 'How high?'—*on the way up*." (Italics in the original.) Such attitudes are, I am sure, distasteful to most Wiccans.

I believe that one's identification as a Witch ought to be self-imposed and based on a personal relationship with the archetypal deities we call the God and the Goddess. On an individual level, everything else, including "Craft law," is purely window dressing; the Gods will teach you what you need to know, or find someone for you who can. For instance, long before I knew, or cared, what "Witchcraft" was, I was initiated by the Goddess in her little-known Nabataean aspect of Atargatis, a bottle-nose dolphin. A series of profound experiences caused me to re-define this dolphin as "human" in spirit if not in form. That set me apart from most of the rest of humanity.

Years later, Seafoam introduced me to the basic tenets of Witchcraft. When she told me, "All acts of love and pleasure are rituals to the Goddess," I had a revelation. Unlike the patriarchal religions, Wicca did not condemn my experience out-of-hand! It asked, instead, the motivation of my actions, which was love. I was sold.

I say if you call yourself a Witch, you are a Witch until proven otherwise, and even if I choose to run the other way I cannot look the other way.

The public domain, however, is the realm of image and politics, and here things get grayer still. Obviously the abusive coven was ripe for expulsion from the Craft community and the inevitable consequences. Other areas, for instance use of sacraments, degree of coven openness, and details of initiation rituals, are much more subject to interpretation. Here one has to take the public—yes, public—perception into account.

Need I say that we, as Witches, have a humongous public-relations problem? One of the bloodiest, most terrifying and most successful propaganda campaigns in human history, launched five hundred years ago and continuing to this day, invests the very name of our religion with the image of brooding, malignant evil—incorrectly, I hasten to add.

Look, ninety-nine percent of us ask no more of our fellow humans than to be allowed to hold our circles out under the Moon and stars, where we like to be, without being furtive or worrying about getting our brains blown out by Jehovans. This is more than just a wish; under the U.S. Constitution, it is our right as citizens!

Contrary to what some people in the Craft have said about me, I have never advocated that "everybody ought to be out of the broom closet." What I have said—and mean, with a vengeance—is that those who choose to remain in the broom closet relinquish their power to shape the public image of Wicca to those of us who are out of the broom closet—and those legions who would defame us.

I have fought on this public-relations front for years, often against other Wiccans who choose not to understand me. In fact I can honestly—and sorrowfully—say I have encountered more hostility from my fellow Wiccans and Pagans than from any other group.

The hostility of non-Wiccans, however, has been far more serious. Years after Seafoam and I left the apartment in Portland, a couple of erstwhile neighbors brought charges against me of sexually and ritually abusing their daughter. I made a clean breast of my Wiccan beliefs to the investigating Oregon State Police officers, who suggested that if I passed a lie detector test, they would drop me from the investigation. I did, and they did, but that was one of the most oppressive and frightening experiences of my life. It is every Wiccan's nightmare to be falsely accused of such monstrosities.

Such experiences have only intensified my desire to promote good public relations for the Craft and understand why, in the minds of so many, we are so hated and feared.

When I undertook to write this article I decided that my opinions, as accurate and well-informed as they might be, were not enough. No, what I needed was some hard data, concrete studies, facts and figures

The social science discipline that deals with group dynamics and the perception of groups by other groups is called sociology. Hence, I tried to find sociological literature on the dynamics of small groups in general and Wicca in particular, and it is here that things get complicated. Sociology—what I can make of it anyhow, having a decidedly anti-academic turn of mind—illuminates many of our public-relations problems and gives us examples of what will and will not work to close the communications gap between "us" and "them."

Take a fictitious example. Jana is a typical Wiccan working at a mundane job; she wears her pentagram inside her shirt. Her friends and co-workers like her and respect her, but think her a little…odd. When the office chatter turns to "witchcraft," as it is wont to do, say, at Hallowe'en, Jana's co-workers show the usual crappy attitudes: fear or ridicule.

This gets to Jana. She wonders what would happen if she came out of the broom closet to them. Her reasoning goes, "They know I'm a good person, and I'm a Witch, so maybe if I come out they'll understand that most Witches are all okay like me, and they won't be so derogatory." In other words, she hopes her co-workers will use inductive logic, reason from the specific to the general, and that their opinions of Wicca will improve. Therefore, one day at the water cooler, Jana shows Mabel, her best office friend, her pentagram. Mabel is, of course, surprised if not shocked.

Do her opinions of Wicca improve? Sociology says, sadly, no. Even if Mabel does not run screaming off into the night and remains friends with Jana, a compensating mechanism takes place which retains the defamatory opinion of Wicca, but makes an exception for Jana.[6] "Oh, Jana! What's a nice girl like you doing mixed-up in that business?" Mabel is likely to ask.

Jana's plan has backfired. A better strategy would be to leave her pentagram in her shirt and use reasonable arguments to attempt to sway her co-workers' opinions without exposing herself unnecessarily.

Sociology offers insights into some of the more puzzling questions that confront us.

Proselytizing versus Self-Dedication

Proselytizing is almost unknown in the Neopagan traditions. Indeed, quite the opposite; I was taught that an aspirant had to ask three times before being accepted as the student of a coven. (Even Seafoam, who was at that time my lover, made me ask three times.)

One might look at what goals these two different processes achieve. Active proselytizing, such as that practiced by most Christian churches, seems to achieve a large number of lightly committed members (lack of regular church attendance among the "faithful" is constantly bemoaned by Christian clergy, particularly in the ecumenical 1990s), a small number of highly committed members, and a very small number of intensely committed clergy, who compose their own subgroup. The formation is a pyramid.

Wicca, on the other hand, is composed of a relatively large group of highly committed members—the Witches— and a small group of people seeking initiation. Unlike a church, most covens have more clergy than initiates. The formation is an inverted pyramid.

I have no statistics on this, but few if any people, once committed to the Craft, seem to drop out. They may, if they get disgusted enough with Craft politics, retreat into solitary practice, but I have, in fifteen years, encountered only one person who said she had relinquished Wicca—a scientist who, I suspect, joined for anthropological reasons.

Another example of an ex-Witch might be Eric Pryor, a self-proclaimed San Francisco "witch" who "miraculously" became "converted" to Christianity after attempting to curse a televangelist. Although there is ample reason to suspect that Pryor was a Christian "mole" who adopted the cloak of Wicca to gain access to the Craft, the inability of those who knew and worked with him to detect him as a pseudo-Witch shows what a divergence of attitudes we tolerate under the mantle of "Witchcraft"—sometimes to our detriment.

Findings from a survey[7] I conducted show that only about one in nine respondents who identify themselves as Pagans and/or Witches consider "conversion, influence or indoctrination by a non-family member" to have been a significant factor in their decision to practice Witchcraft, with the majority of respondents listing this as the least important reason, and some not even bothering to mark the box at all.

Since Witchcraft does not attempt to coerce or even influence people into joining and has no motivational mechanisms like the concept of being "freed from a burden of sin" or "fear of eternal damnation" to impel conversion, why do people choose to become Witches? Equal numbers who answered my survey listed the following two reasons:

> "I had arrived intellectually or philosophically at a set of conclusions about the nature of reality and I learned that others called it 'Witchcraft'" (thirty-three percent).

> "Dissatisfied with the belief system I was raised in, I undertook to explore other belief systems and encountered Witchcraft as part of my personal quest" (thirty-three percent).

A third group gave the following reason:

> "I had an overwhelming, transformative personal experience which shook my previous world-view, and in trying to integrate it into my life I stumbled across Witchcraft" (twenty-two percent).

While one might hope for a larger sample than I have as of this writing, these responses indicate that the motivations for becoming a Witch are much more internal than external. People choose to become Witches because of some inner, personal need, not because of external pressure to conform, desire to please others, to reduce a perceived threat, or to feel part of an in-group. This occurs in spite of the fact that ninety percent of respondents list as their first or earliest memory of Witches and Witchcraft "Popular media, i.e. books, television, plays, movies, regardless of how presented or by whom." In previous decades the portrayal of Witches in the popular media was even more uniformly negative than it is now. Therefore, Witches actually have to overcome the results of early anti-Witch propaganda to pursue their faith!

This stands in stark contrast to the monotheistic/patriar-
chal religions, which enjoy widespread support and reinforcement in the cultures they dominate. In the cases of
Christianity and Islam, they are historically well-known for
gaining converts (often from each other) by "fire and steel."
This drive to convert others to one's own belief or make
them suffer the consequences arises out of a pathological
need to control every aspect of one's environment, which in
turn arises out of a fear of yielding to repressed urges,
which arises from internal weakness and insecurity.[8] In
times past it led to mass-psychotic behavior like that exhib-
ited during the Burning Times, when whole villages, even
whole counties in certain European countries, might be
wiped out for their alleged "heresies." A person could be
accused, tortured, tried, and burned alive because, as Z.
Budapest relates of one of her unfortunate ancestors, "A
bale of hay fell off a wagon in front of her house and the
man said, 'You're a witch, you made it happen!'"[9]

The drive to evangelize has led modern Christians to
achieve some laudable results, such as bringing health care
and literacy to underdeveloped countries, albeit usually at
the expense of the natives' aboriginal belief systems, with
their integrated worldview, botanical knowledge, and traditional teachings about the roles of men and women. Any
beneficial results stand in the shadow of the Burning Times,
however, and that is a long and dark shadow indeed.

Why not turn the question around? Instead of asking,
"Why don't Witches proselytize?" let us ask instead, "Why
do the monotheistic/patriarchal religions proselytize?" After
all, proselytizing is hardly a "natural" human activity with a
demonstrably useful goal, like hunting, sex, or basket-

weaving. Proselytizing takes up a great deal of the individual's and the group's energy.

I can think of several reasons to proselytize.

(a) If the proselytes were, by virtue of their belief, in possession of something that markedly improved their life over that of the non-proselyte. An analogy for Christianity might be inoculation against a fatal disease: it confers an undoubtable benefit upon the inoculated. Indeed, such proselytizing for vaccination against smallpox has succeeded in eradicating the disease among humans.

However, all proselytizing religions make it clear that the benefits derived in this life are mostly limited to foreknowledge of the benefits to be obtained in the life hereafter. God being the capricious cuss that He is, a secure, happy life is not necessarily the reward for faith or good works, hence the question prominent among Christians and Jews: "Why me, O Lord?"

The Pagan answer is, "Shit happens! Adapt or die."

To the Wiccan mind, such believers are in effect sold a bill of goods that neither we or they or anyone else can determine if they have collected on.

So we beg the question: "Why proselytize?"

Reason (b) might be to accumulate brownie points with God. Souls saved are like pieces captured in a chess game; if white has them, black can't get them. The skillful player gets a big reward from the chessmaster, but again, in the next life—see reason (a).

This leads to reason (c), the third and probably most realistic reason why some religions proselytize: the necessity of ever-increasing mutual support.

The book *When Prophecy Fails*[10] is a sociological study of the rise and fall of a small fringe group in the 1950s. Based on the prophecies of a couple of what would now be called "channelers," the group's members believed they would be taken aboard flying saucers just before a period of devastating "earth changes" that would destroy, among other things, the Midwestern city where most of them lived.

The authors, who were sociologists at a nearby university, had developed a theory about belief systems. Why is it, they asked, that when people are confronted with evidence that inarguably refutes their cherished beliefs, they become more strongly attached to them instead of giving them up? The authors learned of the saucer group early in its existence and were able to organize a team to covertly study it through most of its brief life span.

At first, when its predictions of disaster and redemption lay months in the future, the group had a very *laissez-faire* attitude about proselytizing. As often as not, the media were rebuffed in their efforts to get interviews with the group's leaders. While the curious were not turned away, there was no concerted attempt made to go out and seek converts to the group's belief.

All that changed after the expected saucer arrival and the predicted floods, earthquakes, and so on failed to materialize. The group immediately began issuing press releases "explaining" the failure as a "preparedness drill" or a "test of faith." While some left the group, others of the founding members went on the lecture circuit to expound their beliefs! This confirmed the authors' hypothesis that the real function of evangelism lies in a psychological quirk of the human mind: when prophecy fails and reality falls short of expectations, true believers deal with the "cognitive dissonance" thus created by seeking converts who will, by their numbers, reinforce the disproven beliefs! Evangelical religion is sort of like the Arlo Guthrie song, "Alice's Restaurant." If one person believes he's God, you have a nut. If two or two hundred people believe he's God, you have a cult. However, if two million people believe someone is God, well then you have a religion.

The authors of *When Prophecy Fails* were, I believe, aware of the implications of their work for the evangelical religions, but were sensitive enough to the issues of their time (this was right after the McCarthy "witchhunts" for Communists in the government, after all) not to raise them.

To understand the implications, put yourself in the place of Sue, an evangelical Christian. The Bible assures her that someday Christ will return, putting to right all the evils on the Earth and bringing with Him an end to human history. Sue is assured that, because of her faith in Christ as savior, she will be redeemed and experience external positive stimuli, while those who do not share her belief will be condemned and endure unending negative stimuli. With a few crank exceptions, no one can predict the day or hour of Christ's return.[11] Therefore, Sue wakes up every morning hoping that today could be the Second Coming. She lives with this thought through the day. Around about bedtime, however, she realizes that Christ didn't make it. She feels disappointed. Oh well. Maybe while she sleeps. Maybe tomorrow. Surely tomorrow!

For Christians, and other evangelical, eschatological religions, prophecy fails on a daily basis. The long-awaited Second Coming or its equivalent never comes. The promise given two thousand years ago is broken every day. The evangelical Christian (or Shiite Moslem or Jew) goes forward in hope, but also in disappointment. The most potent weapon against the disappointment of a belief system that promises salvation but never delivers is reinforcement. The most potent reinforcement is belief shared with others of the same persuasion who can offer support and comfort.

In one sense, then, every proselytizing religion is facing the failure of its fundamental prophecy: the world is imperfect. Their response is to exhort the power of (their) god to rule our lives, to make us all believe, act, and pray the way they do. The very intangibility of the Christian god, the fact of the absence of Jesus in corporeal form from earthly affairs, is a fundamental failure of Christianity that drives proselytizing. So is the inculcated belief that we are all to blame for His death, even though—paradoxically—it is said He came here expressly as a sacrifice, to die for our sins.

It is an odd paradox that the shakier the belief, the greater the need for reinforcement and evangelism. One can apply the same conclusion to Communism, which shared many common features with Christianity—deified founding figures, professed desire to do good, eschatological ideology, and an intolerance of competing belief systems. Like Christians and Muslims, Communists evangelize with fire and steel—Molotov cocktails and Kalashnikovs. That's what a little war called Vietnam was about.

Now let's contrast Christianity with the Wiccan belief system. Instead of a terminal, eschatological ideology we have one rooted in recurrent cycles of life and death and life, creation and destruction. There is no supernatural "end" to history. Our Witch, Jana, wakes up in the morning not wondering if she will be taken bodily up into heaven today but knowing the Moon will be full in another two days, and that in a fortnight it will be Yule, when the Invincible Sun will be born once again. These events occur with Newtonian regularity, and some of the human race's oldest and most enduring edifices were constructed precisely to establish that regularity, to maintain that connection with the ebb and flow of cosmic forces, never static but always maintaining a dynamic balance between dark and light. The world of the Witch is one in which personal experience of the immanent divine—the sacredness of growing plants, the refreshment of rain, the purifying qualities of frost and fire—is more significant than the credos of "revealed works," more tangible than pie-in-the-sky promises of "salvation."

Christians and other followers of patriarchal religions may experience the beauty of the world as something "put here" for us by the Divine, but not as a manifestation of God, whereas we Witches experience the world as the Goddess manifesting Herself all around us.

Other sociological research has applications to more practical aspects of Wicca.

Faith versus Self-Examination

Every Witch either is clergy or is in the process of becoming clergy, of learning how to create ritual. This necessitates examining the structure and framework of the beliefs of the in-group and subjecting them to critical examination. This is something that most Christians do not do, and in many cases are actually discouraged from doing by their clergy. This examination of self and beliefs is one thing which makes Wicca different from almost every other religion. "Have faith," the others say. "Believe, and ye shall be saved."

Wiccans do not need to "have faith." In fact, we are encouraged not to take things on faith, but to question everything. One can, if one wants to, disbelieve in the Gods as "real outside of oneself." One can, off-circle, question the nature of magic, doubt its validity and effectiveness, so long as one is willing, while in circle, to perform the mental experiment of acting "as if" magic works.

If one's magic is strong, it is assumed it can withstand this type of self-critical enquiry and come out strengthened by it. Those who doubt too often or too deeply should probably find less demanding "faiths."

The Creation of Sacred Space

One of the fundamentals students of the Craft are taught is the creation of "sacred space." Whereas the motivation for constructing an ecclesiastical edifice, the psychological effect of its architecture, its consecration and inhabitation by "holy personages" imbues it with sacrality (the quality of being sacred) in the patriarchal religions, we Witches have a different way of doing things.

Since the Burning Times, when our shrines were overthrown and our sacred groves cut down, our insurance premiums for fires and "acts of God" have gone through the roof. Instead of holding our services in churches, synagogues, and temples, like the patriarchal religions, we have become very adept at "raising the temple" or "casting a circle" wherever we happen to be at the appointed times.

This is the act of creating "sacred space"—a locus that is, in some numinous way, distinct from the space-time around it—is common to all human religions. In Wicca, the space inside our circles is considered to be "between the worlds," i.e., neither part of the consensus reality shared by humans, nor part of the infinite, timeless, *n*-dimensional reality we usually call "the otherworld" where the Gods and other beings exist in non-corporeal forms. The space between the worlds acts as a valve through which thought-forms and probability alterations manifest in consensus reality. Note that in Wicca, as opposed to some forms of ceremonial magic, the circle does not restrain "demons" either on the inside or the outside; rather, it localizes the altered personal space of the Witch, concentrating his or her energy like a plasma bottle in a fusion reactor, while insulating it from external conditions that would diffuse and ameliorate it.

The "reality" of the Witch's circle of power in terms of biophysics would make an interesting study all by itself. Many of us perceive such circles, either visually, by touch or other senses. We observe that some animals also appear to perceive circles. Some of us can detect the residual effects of creating such a circle in a spot, even if it has been taken down. I suspect that we create a faint but real self-sustaining cold plasma torus that could be detected with the appropriate equipment, but I have no way of conducting experiments to test this theory.

Sociologists have studied and proposed different theories about what they call "personal space," the safety zone we carry around with us, and their theories illuminate yet another aspect of the us-them dichotomy. One wears one's personal space like a garment. This is not a metaphor or an allegory or a behavior, but a tangible perception of reality that one can make conscious if one wants to, like the feeling of the clothes you're wearing right now. Feel them?

Sociology has generated two theories about the nature of personal space. The most popular theory, independently proposed by K.B. Little and R. Sommer[12] and thus called "Little-Sommer space," holds that an individual's personal space may be large or small, as indicated by comfortable approach distances. Its boundaries vary with the situation, contracting farther in relation to objects than to persons, and farther in relation to intimate others than to strangers, but any intrusion into one's personal space always elicits a negative reaction.

When I read this description, I knew Little and Sommer had to be a couple of guys, because they had not followed through on the logical absurdity of their hypotheses, namely, that when a woman is making love to a man, her vagina must become "impersonal space" or she would experience a "negative reaction." Presumably, so would he. This theory also invalidates the notion of free will; any intrusion into one's personal space, regardless of who or how or when, always elicits a negative reaction. The only way to avoid it is for personal space to shrink, or for the intruder to become a "nonperson," which denies us our humanity.

Fortunately, there exists another theory of personal space that states that an individual's "reaction to intrusion of others…varies with the particular others who intrude and the circumstances under which the intrusion occurs."[13] In this theory, personal space is more like a permeable field or membrane than a box. An intrusion into one's personal space might be perceived as positive or negative. This is more in accord with the experiences of most Witches, who strive to become adept at evaluating the "energy" of the objects, persons, and events we encounter.

The academicians who put forth these contrasting theories of personal space have their careers invested in them, and experiments too numerous and complex to detail here have been done to confirm one or the other theory, but neither has been proven conclusively. From my experience as a Witch, I propose that both theories are correct—that perceptions of personal space differ with an individual's personality or character.

Authoritarian characters, who would tend to gravitate towards patriarchal religions, experience Little-Sommer space. The boundary of their personal space forms a shield or wall which they retract or extend, depending on the circumstances, but any intrusion into that space meets with a negative reaction.

Those of us in the Craft, who tend to be individualists, experience personal space as a permeable membrane. We receive training in expanding our personal space, even projecting it over distances, which reinforces this perception.

If we acknowledge the perception of Little-Sommer space for at least some people, what happens if this perception succumbs to a mental illness, such as paranoia? Remember, under this hypothesis any intrusion into personal space elicits a negative reaction. What if such a paranoid's personal space becomes pathologically large, especially in relation to individuals perceived as threatening? What if it expands to fill a whole territory—a city or county or country? What if this person is a powerful leader? Why, I think you get a pogrom, Inquisition, Burning Times, or Holocaust.

While the root causes of these events are complex, the instigations of warped individuals cannot be discounted, Torquemada, Spengler and Kramer, Hitler, Stalin, Mao, and Pol Pot—all show an obsession with "evil" in their territories. I contend that, in the same way we Witches perceive the fluctuations of energy in our personal space, so too do the great obsessive tyrants of all time. As their personal space expands to fill their dominions, the perception of anyone different and hence threatening drives them to commit atrocities. They say, "There are still witches out there... I can feel them."

More irons! More wood! More faggots for the fire!

Persuasions of Persuasions

No discussion of the sociology of Witchcraft would be complete without some mention of Tanya M. Luhrmann's *Persuasions of the Witches' Craft.*[14] Unlike almost everyone else who has ever tried to write about our religion, Luhrmann actually joined several English magical groups, looking for the commonalities between Wicca, feminist spirituality, and ceremonial magic. This was sound anthropology, and she is to be commended for it. Luhrmann was trying to understand what made magic appealing to us, the educated, urbane inhabitants of materialistic Western culture. Why should we pursue a path that is not only socially disapproved but flies in the face of the scientific/rationalist paradigm that informs our society? What makes us, in short, different from them?

Luhrmann comes up with several answers. "Magicians [she uses the term inclusively to refer to all her subjects] repeatedly described themselves as having a 'childlike wonder' at the world, a continual surprise at the diversity of nature, and they talk about the need for and value of playful fantasy."[15] This we might describe as a neotonous mindset, neotony being carrying juvenile characteristics into adulthood. Going hand-in-hand with this is the significance of our subjective experience. Luhrmann's observations support the findings of my survey: we are inwardly oriented people.

Another difference is how we confront control issues. According to Luhrmann, "...magic is about power, about controlling and dominating and being dominated or being in service to a higher form, and issues of power are often highly charged in these practitioners' lives."[16]

Luhrmann got quite good at her magical practice. She found herself adopting the attitudes and values of the magicians she worked with, even awakening early one morning to find psychopompic Druids beckoning from her window. It's a damn shame she didn't go on to become a Witch—she would have made a fine one—but after two years' foray into Faery she returned to the world of social science. When she published—and here one detects an almost apologetic tone in her writing—she had to adopt the orthodox anthropological point of view that magic does not work, and since it does not work, what psychological mechanisms allow believers to compensate for the cognitive dissonance their continual failure creates?

Surprisingly, Luhrmann finds it is the practice of magic itself. She suggests that the magician's thought processes "drift" as he or she moves deeper into magical practice. As one practices magic, Luhrmann says, one's intellectual habits change in three outstanding ways:

(a) interpretation of coincidental events as evidence of magical success;

(b) acquisition of new knowledge, categories, and discriminations;

(c) use of new assumptions that alter patterns of thinking and speaking.

She calls this change in one's intellectual habits "interpretive shift." In addition, she says we fail to subject our beliefs to the stringent scientific criteria that could falsify them, a failing that, I am sure, we share with other religions.

Here I must point out a failing that Luhrmann shares with almost every rationalist. She writes, "Modern magic rests upon the idea that thought can affect matter without the intervention of the thinker's acts."[17]

Balderdash, I say.

First, we do act. Whether carefully prepared or spontaneous, a ritual or other magical working is a set of formalized actions performed on a symbolic object with a clear-cut goal in mind. The rationalist has problems with magic because he or she refuses to acknowledge that there can be anything other than a psychological connection between the symbol and the thing it represents, but the fact is we live in a Heisenbergian, quantum-physical universe. Being no physicist herself, Luhrmann discounts these observations when made by magicians.

Second, the notion that we are trying to affect matter is fallacious. I can spend all day willing my athame to rise into the air, but if I want to cut a circle, it is a lot easier to go over and pick it up. I can will a lump of clay to shape itself into a poppet, but it is a lot more efficient to use my hands. When we use magic we are not trying to influence matter, we are almost always trying to influence events—cure an illness, prevent unwanted people from harassing us, make sure a birth goes well, speed up the arrival of that check we have been told is in the mail. Events are matter in motion, in flux. Matter in motion, as the practitioner of martial arts knows, can be deflected in a completely different vector by a very slight application of force. Large, complex events can be profoundly altered by minor, seemingly insignificant, almost intangible factors. This arcane knowledge has become the recently discovered field of chaos theory. Luhrmann totally neglects this fundamental element of magic in her analysis, proving she is no mathematician, either.

Towards the end of her book, Luhrmann hits upon one of the most essential elements of the us-them dichotomy: the function of sacred play in our rituals. "Sacred play is let's-pretend play experienced as divine, sacred, as if pertaining to another real but not-ordinary world: it can be the state of becoming the gods, or interacting with the gods, in which the pretense passes the threshold into vivid reality, the 'really real.'"[18] This ambiguous "as-if" quality about our identities as magicians (or Witches or Pagans), as well as the literal-metaphorical ambiguity of our spells, helps us to rationalize our practice, Luhrmann says, and here she has hit the nail on the head.

Sacred play is one of Wicca's most redeeming features. The popular impression of the Witch as chained to a rote ritual, any deviation from which brings disaster, is, as we might expect, 180 degrees out of phase. We obtain a phenomenal amount of freedom in our spirituality because we evaluate our experience by the results it produces in us, not by its conformance to some formula or doctrine.

Need I say that, if one believes one is acting out the Word of God, and that the fate of all creation ultimately hangs in the balance, one is going to take one's actions very seriously? Performance anxiety sets in. With God as the Almighty, the significance of the individual practitioner dwindles to nothing. To compensate, the significance of one's actions must become huge and absolute. One acts on behalf of a God who is, paradoxically, omnipotent but has no tangible power aside from that of His chosen minions. There is no room for the workings of chance, no scale of grays; you are either doing God's work or the Devil's.

Play, with its unstructured, free-flowing quality, is an anathema to the authoritarian power structures that characterize the patriarchal religions. I say it is precisely because we make a choice to believe, acknowledge our role as creators, as Gods, that we are able to laugh about our religion, joke about the Gods, and at the same time realize that, by our very existence, we are undertaking the terrifically serious work of subverting the dominant paradigm. It is that very levity that allows us to go about the job of changing the universe without being crushed by the responsibility, or becoming dogmatic blatherers, like so many "revolutionaries" of the 1960s. Those among us who see themselves as "chosen by the Gods" seem to have lost the ability to poke fun at themselves, which is the essence of mental health. A grim Witch is Grimm, indeed.

I started this contribution with a cautionary anecdote about the divergence of our beliefs. I would like to end it with a warning against expecting reciprocity.

We, as Witches, revel in diversity and judge others by their acts; therefore, we want to think that the forces opposing us will behave in the same way. It is tempting to believe that, by at least following the Wiccan Rede, or actually performing good works in our communities, we can defeat the falsehoods about us, placate our enemies and turn them into friends.

We must fight the falsehoods at every opportunity, but make no mistake about it, those who would destroy us, the modern-day Inquisitors of the airwaves, do not care what we do; they care what we are, and that is something we cannot change without ceasing to exist. Our existence alone they perceive as a threat to their world. If we are to understand the reasons for this hostility and develop effective ways of combating it, an understanding of the social sciences is as important to us as herbcraft or spells. I hope this contribution has demonstrated that.

Whether we are in or out of the broom closet, we ought to be thankful that we live in a secular society where all religions are guaranteed equal protection under the laws of the land. However, what if we don't take advantage of this situation, unique in human history? What if, instead of exercising this hard-won freedom, we neglect or reject it out of fear, greed, lassitude, or other base motives? It is as if we do not have the freedom at all!

I am reminded of something said to me by an organizer of the Pagan craft fair I mentioned earlier. When asked what upset her about putting these *Witchcraft Today* books on a table in the front of the hall, she yelled, "You can't go around shoving Witchcraft down other peoples' throats!" I had no idea that some books lying on a table amounted to a violation of someone's personal space, but obviously, in the minds of some insecure Witches, it does.

The fundamentalists seeking domination in this country will try to intimidate and terrorize us so that, out of fear, we constrain, defame, expose, and destroy each other. By driving us to subjugate each other, they get us to do their dirty work for them. They have won their war without firing a shot, without needing to write new laws or subvert the First Amendment to destroy us.

When that happens, it is we ourselves who become the warlocks of the new Burning Times.

Notes

1. My pseudonyms. Not their real names, Craft names, inner or outer court names, or anything like that.

2. J. Douglas and F. Waksler, *The Sociology of Deviance* (Boston: Little, Brown and Co., 1982).

3. Personal correspondence.

4. No such Navajo "tribe" exists. White Sands is hundreds of miles from the traditional Navajo homeland. Navajos whom I know suggest that Bickham was "adopted" by a Navajo family living in White Sands.

5. Christ accepted diversity, preached tolerance, and rejected the phony orthodoxies of his time. I have coined the term "Jehovan" to distinguish between authentic followers of Jesus and self-styled "Christians" who are intolerant, demand conformity, and promote totalitarian religious ideals.

6. Rupert Brown, *Group Processes: Dynamics Within and Between Groups* (Oxford: Basil Blackwell, 1988), 215.

7. For a copy of this survey, send a legal-sized, self-addressed, stamped envelope to In Our Hands Media Project, 1300 West I-40 Frontage, #200-134, Gallup, New Mexico 87301.

8. See, for example, Wihelm Reich, *The Mass Psychology of Fascism* (New York: Farrar, Strauss & Giroux, 1970).

9. Related in the video *Out of the Broom Closet* (In Our Hands Media Project, 1990). To order a copy, send $19.95 plus $3.00 for shipping and handling to the above address.

10. Leon Festinger, Henry W. Riecken and Stanley Schachter, *When Prophecy Fails* (New York: Harper & Row, 1956). Although it has been criticized on the grounds that the sociologists may have unduly influenced the group, *When Prophecy Fails* remains a classic in the field.

11. *The Bible,* Matthew 24:36.

12. Marvin E. Shaw, *Group Dynamics: The Psychology of Small Group Behavior* (New York: McGraw-Hill, 1971), 119-130.

13. Ibid, 120.

14. T.M. Luhrmann, *Persuasions of the Witch's Craft* (Oxford: Basil Blackwell Ltd., 1989).

15. Ibid, 103.

16. Ibid, 104.

17. Ibid,117.

18. Ibid, 333–334

About the Author

Malcolm Brenner is a survivor of Orgonomy, the 1960s, and his English mother's cooking. He had planned to be Steven Spielberg, but couldn't stand Los Angeles. He learned Dianic/Eclectic Witchcraft from his first wife, Seafoam, with whom he produced the Eleusinian Harvest Festival, the Pacific Northwest's first large Pagan gathering, in 1981. They also published a few issues of *MaidenSpirit Journal,* the first Northwestern Pagan digest.

The founder of In Our Hands Media Project, a small, helpless organization that does whatever he wants it to, Brenner has produced two Pagan video documentaries, *Out of the Broom Closet* (1990) and *Robert: Portrait of a Witch* (1991). His remarkable photographs grace the previous three books in the *Witchcraft Today* series. He works as a reporter and lives with his best-ever wife Vera, 2.5 children, three dogs, and two cats on the Navajo reservation in New Mexico, where he says, "Shi dooda adilgashii, shikis."

When Sex is a Sacrament:

Sexuality Between the Worlds

By Rhiannon Asher

Pass the word and pass the Lady
Pass the plate to all who hunger
Pass the wit of ancient wisdom
Pass the cup of crimson wonder...

Jethro Tull, *Songs from the Wood*

Standing erect and colorful in our garden is a May Pole, a bright icon that is central to our religion, and one that sets us far apart from the religions of the masses. The phallic May Pole is an ancient symbol of love, lust, and the life that flows from the union of these sacred emotions. Every Spring, Pagans everywhere dance the May Pole as our ancestors did before us, celebrating the most powerful and primal of forces, our sacred sexuality. The absolute holiness of our sexual, sensual bodies is one of the most wonderful discoveries we make when we find our way back to our Pagan roots. Many Pagans describe their experience of coming home to the Earth as a profound homecoming to their own sacred bodies, as well.

"When I was a Christian, I could not reconcile my sexuality and my spirituality; the two seemed to be very distinct things, with one canceling out the other. I was either a sexual being who couldn't be spiritual, or I was a spiritual being who couldn't be sexual. I seemed always to be floating just above my body, living in my head. When I returned to Paganism, I also found myself joyfully returning to the temple of my body," said Antigone, age forty-two and a practicing Wiccan priestess for almost eight years.

According to Joyce, a forty-four-year-old Witch who describes herself as born Christian, then a non-Christian for twenty-five years, and a Wiccan for the last seven, "My sexuality and my views about myself have changed very radically from back when I was Christian, to when I was agnostic, to when I was an actively seeking Pagan, to when I became Wiccan. As I've discovered the innate value of myself and the Earth, my sexuality has become more free, more full, and more sacred."

Sex is a mystery, one of the greatest of all mysteries. It is at once common and rare. It is a pleasurable physical act that most adults have experienced; it is also an amazing spiritual high that many sexually active adults in this society never reach. Sex is a celebration and exploration of the most primal of forces, forces that create life from life by rising from our dark centers and filling us with an intense desire for union. As with all mysteries, sex is often experienced on many levels at once. It is sublime lovemaking, a way of worshiping one another and the Gods that moves us out of our separate selves into the ecstasy of oneness. In sex, we are truly one with our lovers, as close to another human being as we can ever be, outside of our mother's womb. Sex is animalistic and powerful, flesh against flesh in the overwhelming heat of passion.

Sex is not sanitary and neat and free from danger, not if it's honest. Sex can shake us to our core, sending us to the edge of madness in our desire for its pleasures. It is wild and unpredictable, an act and an attitude of surrender to forces that are much larger than we are—forces we fear, yet find ourselves eagerly beckoning to us with our trembling bodies. We want to hear Her offer us "My lips, blood-red, that can at one imperial kiss drain out the rendered soul from your body, and give it back so dyed with the taste of Me that from now until your death you shall seek Me ever...."[1] It is in our surrender, paradoxically, that we find our essential power; we cannot love with our entire beings and remain afraid of life.

According to Georg Feuerstein in *Sacred Sexuality: Living the Vision of the Erotic Spirit,* "Sacred sex, which is the experience of ecstasy, is the real sexual revolution."[2] In sexual ecstasy, we find our greatest authenticity and power, because we are face to face with one another, naked and unashamed. People sometimes describe sexual ecstasy as a dream state; beyond that phrase, there are often no words to describe it. It is an altered state of great transformation and wonder, and those who have experienced it seek to enter it again and again. To enter the realms of sexual ecstasy (realms that are as dark as they are bright) we must emulate Inanna on Her journey to the Underworld; we must lay aside all our physical trappings—clothing, jewels and ego—and enter with nothing but our essential selves.

We find that when we enter this bright darkness with nothing but honesty, we are given so much that our hearts and our spirits can hardly contain it.

Sex is fun; when experienced in a state of innocence and discovery, it is a joyful and playful way to bond with another. In the film *Henry & June*, Anais Nin exclaims as she contemplates her sexual nature, "I feel so innocent!"[3] Sex feels good, within our bodies and our hearts, and no amount of sex-negative propaganda can convince us that something that feels so good can be bad. Sex can be dangerous; in this age of AIDS and other sexually transmitted diseases we cannot be sexual beings and not know of the physical dangers inherent in this act of love. Therefore we learn to love safely, but we continue loving. Sex can be dangerous in other ways as well, for it transforms us in ways we may not predict and may not think we are ready for. It is dangerous, for it sometimes sends us outside our formerly content lives, seeking the fulfillment of desires that we may not have known we had within us. However, the act that creates life and bonds us one to the other is not evil.

Sex is worship. In sex we kneel before the sacred altars of life. The yoni is the Holy Grail from which we drink; the phallus is the magick wand that sparks us with fire. When we kneel at those altars with reverence, we come face to face with our own and our lover's divinity. In our loving, we seek in one another's eyes the shine of the sacred, the ancient and ineffable glance of the God/dess. In the song "The Return of Pan" by the Waterboys, the lines: "The Great God Pan is alive/It's possible to look into His immortal eyes"[4] do not just refer to a deity outside us. The Great God Pan and the Great Goddess Aphrodite can be found where they have always been, within ourselves and our

lovers. Sex is the sacred act from which all life flows; wh
we love one another in this way, we are creating as the
Gods. If it harm none, there is no part of our sexual beings
and our sexual lives that is anything less than holy. However, if sex is turned into an act of aggression, or done without awareness or consideration of our lover's needs and
desires, it is blasphemy.

These are some of the beliefs and attitudes that Pagans
hold about sexuality, attitudes that many of us have only
discovered since finding the Pagan path. We all grew up in
this sex-negative culture, hearing mixed messages about sex
all our lives. Our parents and the church simply told us,
"Don't do it—it's sinful and dangerous unless it happens
between married people." Hollywood and the media gave
us entirely different messages, from Elvis suggestively
rolling his pelvis on dinner-time TV in the 1950s, to
Madonna, the Playboy Channel, and 1-900 sex lines on
late-night television in the 1990s. Many of us grew up confused, and painfully aware of our dilemma. We either con-
formed and abstained, or we cast all restraint to the wind
and ran into the enticing and deadly arms of the beast. We
were told that in choosing the pleasures of the flesh over
the purity of the spirit we were risking our eternal souls,
but we knew (deep inside, if not as conscious thought) that
in denying the flesh, we were denying life. Sex is energy—
life energy. We knew that when we stopped making love,
we would accelerate the process of dying.

The sexual revolution of the 1960s and 1970s provided
choices and opportunities that would shape us in ways that
we could not predict. While we became more free to
explore alternative lifestyles and experiences that had previously been taboo, our new freedoms also brought diseases

the potential to devastate our culture,
emotionally. As we moved through
se that followed, we found ourselves
.. our dusty old Judeo-Christian cloaks to
..brace a more humanistic and realistic sexual ethic, but
often at the expense of our spirituality. We knew that sex
was a natural thing, but often we forgot that it was more
than simply a physical release. In our desire to fully experience our sensual, sexual selves, many of us treated sex as if
it was not a spiritual act at all. Consequently, we treated one
another as sexual objects to be used for our own selfish
pleasure. For some Pagans, it was our eventual realization
of the purity and spirituality of sex that guided us to this
life-affirming path and keeps us walking upon it.

Pagans understand that our bodies are made of the same
elements that make up the sacred Earth, and thus are
absolutely holy. There is no part of us that is unclean or
shameful. Our bodies are beautiful, magickal works of art,
regardless of their shapes and sizes. When new Pagans see
the ease with which many Pagans move in their bodies and
touch one another, they are sometimes frightened, and
often intrigued. They have come from a culture in which
sexuality is either denied and repressed or flaunted. Sex is
not often seen as a natural and beautiful expression of our
spirituality, although there are always some who catch a
glimpse of this truth. Sex is spirit and spirit is sex. It is all
vital and creative energy, the energy that binds the universe
together and keeps us spinning through space.

Pagans worship lusty Old Gods like Pan, Aphrodite, and
Inanna, Bacchus, Venus, and Dumuzi. Our Gods are not
asexual and pristine; they are sensual and sexual. Sex is the
primal act that creates life—life as another sentient being,

or simply life as more energy, more love, more peace in the world. If this is so in the worlds of nature, would it not also be so in the worlds of spirit? As above, so below. The Gods birthed us in Their own images, They would not have given us the ability to feel such great and overwhelming pleasure unless They knew the value of the gift.

Our pre-Judeo-Christian ancestors knew the joys of sex without the guilt that distorts it into something ugly. Before the warring nomads swept across the Earth, leaving in their wake dead men and motherless children, and taking as slave brides as many young women as they could carry away, sex was a sacrament. In some Goddess temples, hundreds of priestesses gave themselves in sacred sexual service to spiritual seekers who had come to worship the Great Goddess at Her living altars. In the humble homes and fertile fields of common people, lovers tumbled lustily in one another's arms, never dreaming that one day pious old men would declare this natural and pleasurable act of love to be the greatest of all evils.

There is much evidence that sex was once recognized and honored as a spiritual act, before all the distortions it would later endure at the hands of celibate priests, or husbands and fathers who controlled their wealth by controlling their wives and daughters. One of the oldest pieces of writing in existence was found in the temple of the great Sumerian Goddess Inanna. It is a beautiful and very sexual love poem from Inanna to Dumuzi, Her lover and consort. In this poem She calls Him "the one my womb loves best," and tells Him to "plow my vulva, oh man of my heart, plow my vulva."[5] Even the Bible still contains the obviously sexual Song of Songs (or Song of Solomon) that contains such verses as "Let him kiss me with the kisses of his mouth: for his love is better than wine;" "A bundle of myrrh is my well-beloved unto me; he shall lie all night betwixt my breasts;" and "His left hand is under my head and his right hand does embrace me."[6] Although many embarrassed clergymen have long asserted that this strangely different book of the Bible is really a long metaphor about the love between Jesus and the Church, objective readers would probably surmise that it is exactly what it appears to be: a celebration of sacred sexual love.

Although not every Pagan understands the spiritual significance of sex and approaches lovemaking with an attitude of worship, many do. As in every other population of people, the Pagan community has its share of misogynists, misfits, egotists, and those who are confused about sexuality. In Goddess religions, there is a smaller percentage of misogynists than in the larger population, but they do exist. We were all born and raised in this dysfunctional culture, and it takes some of us longer to heal and to find our sexual/spiritual power than it takes others.

Since Pagans often celebrate sexuality as part of their spirituality, new Pagans (and non-Pagans) may confuse this celebration with promiscuity. Most seasoned Pagans who understand the power and responsibilities of sex are not promiscuous, although they may not confine their sexual experience to only one lover (or they may—contrary to popular belief, many Pagans are happily monogamous). However, in the Pagan community there is probably a larger-than-average number of alternative relationships, as people feel more free to explore lifestyles that the larger culture might judge to be immoral or unnatural. Any survey among Pagans would probably turn up a fairly large number of open marriages, triads, and other multi-partner arrangements. Many gays, lesbians, and bisexuals are also drawn to the Pagan path and find themselves fitting very comfortably into our community. Just as Pagans question authority when it comes to religious matters, they also often question authority when it comes to matters of the body and the heart. Pagans are an intelligent, curious, rebellious lot, and we often find the constraints of societal norms to be too limiting to our spiritual growth. Many Pagans actively design their relationships to fit their unique needs and desires, rather than try to fit into someone else's mold.

"I have two lovers who are also one another's lovers, and I can't tell you how blessed I feel," Antigone said. She is a Witch and a member of a thriving triad of two women and one man, a relationship choice that is becoming more and more common within the Pagan community. "There is so much love in our house that friends comment on the peace they feel when they visit us. When I make love with Arthur, I know I'm making love with the gentle and sensual Horned God—but now I am also nurtured by the loving arms of the Goddess as well."

"Pagans don't follow any one authority, unless it is the wisdom of Nature," John, a thirty-five-year-old Druid, said. "In Nature, we see the most diversely beautiful sexual acts. Animals don't need laws to tell them how to love each other. They just follow their instincts, their inner voices."

In a religion that recognizes that the Gods are sexual beings who are honored by the sacred sexual loving of Their children, we are freed from much of the sexual dysfunction that plagues many of our non-Pagan neighbors. Pagans do not have a lot of sexual rules, except that we harm none (including ourselves). Although some newly realized Pagans may go through a period of sexual excess as they discover themselves to be in a community of sexually free people, they usually find their balance as they learn and grow. Most Pagans are strong advocates of safe sex practices. We know that we live in dangerous times, when people can literally die from loving, and we are not willing to take that risk with ourselves and our lovers. However, we know that if we live our sexual lives with awareness, and approach one another honestly and with respect and reverence, however we choose to express ourselves sexually is absolutely holy.

Pagan attitudes toward the body are exemplified by the Five-Fold Kiss, a Wiccan blessing with which many Pagans are familiar. The Five-Fold Kiss is a Gardnerian-based rite that is often given and received by the Priestess and Priest in Full Moon rituals, initiations, and elevations. It is usually done formally, standing up, without much sexual feeling and is performed more as a humbling and honoring rite than a sexual one. The formal words spoken as we kiss the feet, knees, phallus/yoni (or womb), breasts and lips of another are as follows (of course, there are variations, depending on the tradition):

> *Blessed be thy feet that have brought*
> *   thee in these ways;*
> *Blessed be thy knees that kneel before*
> *   the sacred altars;*
> *Blessed be thy yoni/phallus, without*
> *   which we would not be;*
> *Blessed be thy breasts, formed in beauty*
> *   and in strength;*
> *Blessed be thy lips, that speak the*
> *   sacred names.*

In our workshops we teach lovers to lie down together and honor one another with this rite, kissing and touching and holding one another erotically and lovingly as they speak their blessings from their hearts. Sometimes participants are moved to tears by this exercise; as Witches and Earth people, they have long known sex to be sacred, but in this rite they experience the sacredness directly. For those who are still confused by the cultural dichotomy of spiritual versus sexual, this simple exercise can bring a deepening of understanding of how absolutely sacred our sexuality is. When we sensually kiss one another's sex, saying "Blessed be thy yoni (or phallus), without which we would not be," we are kneeling before the sacred altars and expressing a central mystery of Wicca, the mystery of Life itself.

In the larger society, women especially receive some pretty negative messages about their bodies and about their sexuality. We all have grown up with the "madonna/whore" dichotomy, the messages that teach us that "the good girls go to heaven, but the bad girls go everywhere."[7] Many of us have found ourselves standing at the crossroads, having to decide whether to choose vibrant life here and now on this green Earth (with hell to pay later), or life in some sterile hereafter (with our warm bodies to deny now). Joyce talks about the artificial separation of the sacred and the sensual, of God and Nature, in traditional Christian teachings and how these ideas affected her and changed as she found her Pagan path:

> The whole cultural environment of Christianity—
> Catholicism specifically—is the denial of anything
> physical as having value. Value came from outside; it
> was never from within. Either God gave you grace, or
> you did something 'good' to achieve approval from out-

side yourself, which gave you value for that period of time. There was no innate value of the person, and anything that had to do with the physical was bad: eliminating body wastes was bad, having no clothes on was bad, the skin was bad, the flesh was bad. Spirituality was way out of there; it was something you could only attain with the help of someone else. I was so totally sucked into the lack of self-value that I didn't even realize it until I began to come out of it. I thought that I had no guilt, that I didn't feel guilt, until I really began not to feel guilt.

As I began to realize and feel the infinite value of all things physical—me, other people, the world, everything around me, energy—my life began to change. As I let go of some of these beliefs, I became more free to see the profane and the sacred as the same thing.

There are many reasons why Pagans understand and experience sex differently than many non-Pagans, but one of the most important differences is something that sets us apart in other ways as well. Most of the influential world religions base their teachings on the concept of transcendence, while Pagans teach and experience our spirituality as one of immanence, of the recognition of divinity within all life. We live in a society that teaches that divinity is "out there somewhere" in ethereal space, not here within our blood and bones and within the rich dark soil of the Earth Herself. The religious environment in which many of us grew up, and which continues to shape society, is an environment of repression and denial of all things physical and earthy. If we can see it, touch it, taste it, feel it, it's sinful, and must be denied and transcended. We have heard fundamentalists describe their devil as "the god of this world" and preach that holiness can only reside outside the natural world.

Many people spend their lives trying to come to terms with this impossible dichotomy. Some get married and seek sexual and emotional fulfillment within the marriage—often with minimal success, judging by the high divorce rates in our society. Others become sex addicts who use and abuse one another, believing that if we are not good (as defined by some church), we must be bad—and if what we are doing is bad anyway, it really does not matter how we treat one another while we do it. According to this mindset, sex is merely a physical need, with no emotional or spiritual components at all. Still others repress their sexual feelings, choosing spirituality over sexuality, never awakening to the truth that many Pagans come home to in our beautiful, life-affirming religion: sex is spiritual and is the highest form of worship, and we are spiritual and sexual, both at the same time.

As Earth-worshiping Pagans, we understand our spirituality and our lives to be part of a great organic whole, as natural as sunshine and moonlight and the tides of the sea. We were not spoken into existence by an asexual male god who lives elsewhere and judges us for feeling and expressing our natural sensual desires. We were created by the sacred sexual union of our flesh-and-blood mothers and fathers, and born in a great gush of blood and water, children of the Earth, all of us. Thus we celebrate divinity within ourselves and all of Nature, knowing that everything alive is holy and worthy of respect and reverence.

As our ancestors were before us, we are a lusty, earthy people, at home in our bodies and on the Earth. Our sexuality is central to our worship and our world view. Our rituals are rich with sexual symbolism, from the May wreath and the bright, be-ribboned May Pole to the chalice and the blade. Our Goddess charges us to "Let My worship be in the heart that rejoices, for behold, all acts of love and pleasure are My rituals." We were not born in sin, we were born in love, and Pagans celebrate that love in our rituals and our lives.

Jason is an articulate and mature sixteen-year-old Pagan whose mother and stepfather are Pagan. He describes himself as a bisexual teenager who has been sexually active for a couple of years. "My mother never really says a lot about sex, except that it's a beautiful and magickal thing. She also says it's kind of a pointless thing when there's no love involved, and that when there is love, it's amplified…and she's right. But beyond that, she really doesn't impose her views. I've figured out a lot for myself."

When asked how his sexual views differ from those of his non-Pagan peers, he says that he feels sorry for many young people who are experiencing the physical act of sex without opening themselves to love and emotion. "The mass media portrays women as objects to be looked at and sex as a really great thing that you want to get as much of as you can all the time. I would say to young people who buy into this that you are missing out on a lot, you're missing more than half the picture. A lot of people seem to be just out there having sex because it's fun, without feeling the love and emotions that are the best and most important part of lovemaking."

Jason describes his sexuality as being strongly influenced by his spirituality, because his spirituality has taught him to love and respect himself and others.

To people who know that modern Pagans base many of our traditions and practices on the traditions and practices of ancient fertility religions, but know little else about us, our emphasis on the sacredness of sexuality and of the body may seem perverse and strange. Pagans often work skyclad in rituals, and it is not unusual to see Pagans dancing naked around fires at summer festivals. We are sometimes rumored to have orgies in our circles, rumors that for most of us are not true at all. Although our Goddess tells us, "As a sign that you be truly free, you shall be naked in your rites" and "Sing, feast, dance, make music and love, all in My praise," these words have nothing to do with irresponsible sex, but rather with a healthy respect for the beauty and magick of the physical body. When we stand or dance naked before one another and the Gods, we do this as an act of trust and innocence. Our ritual nudity is not an invitation to sexual advances, and those who would betray a coven mate's trust in this way would most likely be confronted about their inappropriate behavior.

"Although there is a popular notion that Pagans are somehow loose and immoral—at least according to Christian standards—my experience has been very different," said Keith, a thirty-six-year-old Witch who has been practicing the Craft for twenty years. "The more my Pagan spirituality has developed, the more I've paid attention to the consequences of my behavior on my relationships, and the responsibilities that are inherent in my actions. I know that everything I do leaves ripples and wakes in the water. I think that to properly follow 'an ye harm none, do what thou wilt' tends to make one a much more moral and ethical person sexually than whatever our popular brand of

Christianity seems to be teaching—which is mostly 'pretend like you're not doing it and lie about it if you are.'"

However, Great Rites—ritual acts of sexual intercourse—do occur, but usually in private between established lovers. To people raised on church and media ideas of spirituality and sexuality, it may seem strange to think of lovers casting a circle and invoking Gods into their own and each other's bodies before lovemaking. To those of us who regularly explore the sexual mysteries, ritual sex is truly the highest act of worship. It is in the primal act of sexual union that we most closely approach the mysteries of life and death and rebirth. The French call orgasm "the little death" for good reason. When we are in the throes of sexual ecstasy, our egos dissolve into the nothing and everything of Oneness, a momentary Oneness that is perhaps a foreshadow of the Void that we enter upon physical death. Paradoxically, it is also in the egoless state of sexual ecstasy that we feel most alive. Sex can also be used to enhance our magick. When working a healing or prosperity spell, sending energy raised during lovemaking is a powerful way to seal the spell.

Although group sex within Pagan rituals is largely a myth perpetuated by those who fear us, ours is a fertility religion, and our rituals are often ripe with sexual symbolism. For example, most Pagan rituals, regardless of the tradition, end with a sharing of food and drink, and in many traditions, the wine is blessed with a "symbolic Great Rite," a dipping of the athame into the chalice of wine or juice, with the Priestess and the Priest saying words such as the following:

> *Be it known*
> *that a man is not greater than a woman,*
> *nor is a woman greater than a man;*
> *For what one lacks the other may provide.*
> *As the athame is to the male,*
> *so is the chalice to the female,*
> *and conjoined they bring happiness in truth.*
> *For there is no greater magick in all the world*
> *than that of love.*[8]

Depending on the time of year, sexual symbolism is often part of Pagan rituals. Ours is an Earth religion, and we honor and celebrate the seasonal changes, the flowing of life into death and death into life once more. We base our rituals on actual changes in nature, not on arbitrary mythological events or obscure doctrine. Our rituals make sense as they follow, emulate, and celebrate the natural world. Our Wheel of the Year mythology goes something like this (with variations, depending on the tradition one follows):

Samhain (October 31): Our God has died and returned to the womb of the Great Mother, where He grows strong and awaits His rebirth at Yule. This is the time of the greatest darkness, the time of the Crone, the ancient Queen of the Dead. In the natural world, life is decaying into death, returning nutrients to the soil that will bring life again in the Spring. Since Pagans are lovers of paradox, we often find great power in celebrating life at the apex of death; as we speak the names of our beloved dead and light candles in their honor, we may be drawn to make love in the flickering candlelight. Samhain is a time to honor death by affirming life.

Yule/Winter Solstice (December 21): The Great Mother gives birth to the Sun Child, and light returns to the Earth once more. Yet we have just come through the great darkness, and the Earth still lies frozen under a blanket of snow. In the natural world, plants and animals still sleep, although their dreams grow more active and colorful as they begin to move toward wakefulness. Our rites often happen in two parts: we observe a longest night vigil, watching by the side of our Mother as She labors to give birth, and then we rise before daybreak to brave the cold and welcome the Sun's rebirth.

Imbolc/Imbolg/Candlemas (February 2): The Sun Child plays happily as He grows toward manhood. His Mother still nourishes and nurtures Him, while She grows younger and more vibrant with each passing day. In the natural world, seedlings stir beneath the ground, and hibernating animals begin to awaken and share warmth with one another in the Winter cold. Sexual fires are beginning to burn and the warmth awakens the sleepers. This is the beginning of the sexual season. At this time, we celebrate our first Spring rite, although it may still look like Winter to the casual observer. Our circles are brightly lit with candles and the promise of Spring.

Ostara/Vernal Equinox (March 20): The Sun God is a beautiful adolescent who is infatuated by the lovely Spring Maiden, our Mother who has grown young again in the Spring rains. The two young lovers begin to move toward one another, their hearts and their bodies longing to touch and blend as one. Everywhere in Nature animals couple, swell with life, and give birth, while plant life begins to bud and blossom. This is a chaotic, sensual time, the time of the courtship of the Goddess and the God. Our rites are bright with symbols of fertility: seeds, colored eggs, and spring flowers.

Beltane (May 1): This is the time of the Sacred Marriage of the Lady and the Lord. They have both reached sexual maturity and are ready to consummate and celebrate their love for one another. In the natural world, life is abundantly birthing and blossoming, as the Earth warms beneath the heat of the Sun and ripens beneath the Spring rains. Our rites are celebrations of sexuality—our own and that of the Lord and the Lady. This is when we dance the phallic May Pole, weaving the streaming ribbons of life together, as the yonic wreath descends in the ultimate act of consummation. This is also a time when many Pagans perform the Great Rite with their lovers, celebrating with their hearts and their bodies the sacred act from which all life flows.

Litha/Summer Solstice (June 21): The Sun God reaches His zenith of power, as He and our Lady joyfully consummate again and again their sacred union. In the natural world, the Earth is abundant and green and flowing with nectar, as Pagans everywhere dance barefoot on the Earth. However, as the Wheel turns, life turns. As the great Sun peaks in power, He immediately begins to wane, to move toward darkness and rest once more. In our rites, we celebrate His power and Her abundance, even as we momentarily feel the chill of Winter as a premonition in our bones. Summer Solstice is a strongly sexual time, as we celebrate the passions of life in the green summer meadows.

Lughnasadh/Lammas (August 2): As the Sun God wanes in the heavens, His essence ripens in the corn, colors the wheat amber and makes ready for His death. Our sexuality takes on more of a languid feel in the hot August days and nights. There is almost a bittersweet taste to our kisses as we prepare for the coming darkness while still celebrating summer with our hearts and our bodies. In many traditions, the Sun God dies at this time, a willing and noble sacrifice. He returns as the first and the finest of fruits to the Great Mother who gave Him life. It is at this point that She turns from His lover to His destroyer, as She wields the sickle that cuts Him down. She then takes Him into Herself again, the ultimate act of consummation of Their holy union.

Mabon/Autumnal Equinox (September 21): This is a time of balance, a time of a fluid interplay between day and night. Lovers often find Mabon to be a magickal time for loving, as the light gives way to darkness and the air smells of wood smoke. There is a cool crispness in the air that brings an urgency to our loving, an indirect, silvery quality to the light that speaks of the darkness to come. According to many traditions, the Bright Lord died at Lughnasadh and now rests in the great womb of the Mother, awaiting rebirth. In other traditions, He dies at the Equinox, cut down by His Dark Twin at the moment of balance. Regardless of the tradition, His brightness has been covered by the darkness, and even as He returns to the Goddess as seed and potential, His Dark Self makes love with Her with dark potency. At Mabon, there is a maturity and wisdom to our loving, a deep understanding that even in our joyous union, death stirs and cannot forever be denied. This is a time to appreciate the abundance of now, to love intensely as if we are loving for the last time and building memories to carry us through the darkness to come.

As we turn with the Earth around the Year Wheel, sex and death are recurring themes in our rites, just as these two forces play like light and shadow through our lives. It makes perfect sense that Beltane and Samhain are half a year apart. Beltane celebrates and honors life, as Samhain celebrates and honors death, and these two Mysteries are opposite, of the same turning sphere; when the one is in ascendancy, the other is in decline.

Starhawk, one of modern Paganism's most influential writers, affirms in her writing the role that sex plays in our spiritual lives: "In Witchcraft, sex is a sacrament, an outward sign of an inward grace. That grace is the deep connection and recognition of the wholeness of another person. In its essence, it is not limited to the physical act— it is an exchange of energy, of subtle nourishment, between people. Through connection with another, we connect with all."[9] Like many Craft writers, she sees no division between our sexuality and the rest of our lives. She teaches techniques for re-linking the different aspects of our lives into one organic whole. In *The Fifth Sacred Thing*,[10] her futuristic novel, the characters are so spiritually and sexually free that many are bisexual and many have several lovers with whom they have deep and lifelong bonds.

In a society that has forgotten many of the ancient truths, that has removed itself so far from Nature that many urban people never walk barefoot on the Earth, never experience the majesty of a forest (and therefore, are often apathetic about the desecration of the environment), the idea of sex as holy communion often seems strange and somehow dangerous. To Pagans who worship in this way, it is the most natural and healing thing they do together. Divinity is not "out there" in some ethereal heaven, far removed from this green Earth; it resides within our very bodies and surges through us as sexual energy. This is the great creative energy of the Universe, the energy that binds all things together and moves life ever forward. It cannot be regulated and controlled by human law—it is too immense. The Gods do not sit outside Nature and make rules and judgments about our sexual behavior; the Gods move through us in sacred sexual ecstasy. Every sexual encounter that is approached with reverence is a holy, creative act, an act of worship. When Pagans understand and practice these truths, they find that they have truly come home.

In a society in which many people are taking vows of celibacy because the emotional and physical dangers of sex can be too great, many Pagans are making commitments to one or several lovers to be honest and responsible in their loving. We know that sacred sex is not necessarily safe sex, but we also know that sex is too important to our spirituality to repress and deny. Therefore, we kneel humbly and joyfully, and give one another the Five-Fold Kiss, seeking in one another's eyes the clear and untroubled gaze of our beloved God/dess. When we do this, when we approach one another as Deity and sex as worship, we find ourselves speechless before the Mystery. Mystics in every religion have known and tried to teach this truth (and were sometimes killed as heretics for their teachings): we are the Gods, and when we make love with joy, innocence, and power, we are immortal. Sex holds off death, although perhaps not forever. Immortality is living forever in the moment; in sacred sexual ecstasy we are as close to immortality as we will ever be.

Notes

1. "Charge of Drawing Down" from E.R.R. Eddison, *The Mezentian Gate Trilogy* (New York. Dell, 1992 [1935]), 802.

2. Georg Feurstein, *Sacred Sexuality: Living the Vision of the Erotic Spirit* (Los Angeles: Jeremy P. Tarcher, 1992)

3. *Henry & June*, Dir. Philip Kaufman. With Fred Ward, Maria de Medeiros, Uma Thurman, and Richard E. Grant, 1990.

4. The Waterboys, "The Return of Pan," *Dream Harder,* Chrysalis/Ensign, 1993.

5. Diane Wolkstein and Samuel Noah Kramer, *Inanna: Queen of Heaven and Earth* (New York: Harper & Row, 1983).

6. *The Bible,* Song of Songs 1:2, 1:13, 8:3, King James Version.

7. Jim Steinman, "Good Girls Go to Heaven," Meatloaf, *Bat Out of Hell II, Back Into Hell*, MCA Records, 1993.

8. The broken lines indicate the alternating voices of the priestess and priest.

9. Starhawk, *The Spiral Dance* (San Francisco: Harper San Francisco, 1989 [1979]), 111.

10. Starhawk, *The Fifth Sacred Thing* (New York: Bantam Books, 1993).

About the Author

Rhiannon Asher is a Wiccan priestess who lives with her two lifemates and a menagerie of cats, ducks, salamanders, geckos, and fish in Denver, Colorado. She and her partners co-edit *Hole In The Stone*, a quarterly Pagan journal, and *All Acts of Love and Pleasure*, an annual journal of Wiccan and Pagan erotica. Together they teach workshops on sacred sexuality and responsible alternative relationships.

Stay in Touch. . .

Llewellyn publishes hundreds of books on your favorite subjects

On the following pages you will find listed some books now available on related subjects. Your local bookstore stocks most of these and will stock new Llewellyn titles as they become available. We urge your patronage.

Order by Phone

Call toll-free within the U.S. and Canada, **1–800–THE MOON.**
In Minnesota call **(612) 291–1970.**
We accept Visa, MasterCard, and American Express.

Order by Mail

Send the full price of your order (MN residents add 7% sales tax) in U.S. funds to:

> **Llewellyn Worldwide**
> **P.O. Box 64383, Dept. K151-1**
> **St. Paul, MN 55164–0383, U.S.A.**

Postage and Handling

- ◆ $4.00 for orders $15.00 and under
- ◆ $5.00 for orders over $15.00
- ◆ No charge for orders over $100.00

We ship UPS in the continental United States. We cannot ship to P.O. boxes.

Orders shipped to Alaska, Hawaii, Canada, Mexico, and Puerto Rico will be sent first-class mail.

International orders: Airmail—add freight equal to price of each book to the total price of order, plus $5.00 for each non-book item (audiotapes, etc.). Surface mail—Add $1.00 per item.

Allow 4–6 weeks delivery on all orders. Postage and handling rates subject to change.

Group Discounts

We offer a 20% quantity discount to group leaders or agents. You must order a minimum of 5 copies of the same book to get our special quantity price.

WITCHCRAFT TODAY, BOOK ONE
The Modern Craft Movement
edited by Chas S. Clifton

For those already in the Craft, and for those who stand outside the ritual cir-cle wondering if it is the place for them, *Witchcraft Today, Book One* brings together the writings of nine well-known Neopagans who give a cross-sec-tion of the beliefs and practices of this diverse and fascinating religion.

The contributors live in cities, small towns and rural areas, from California to Ireland, and they have all claimed a magical birthright—that lies open to any committed person—of healing, divination, counseling and working with the world's cycles.

Written specifically for this volume, the articles include:

- "A Quick History of Witchcraft's Revival" by Chas S. Clifton
- "An Insider's Look at Pagan Festivals" by Oz
- "Seasonal Rites and Magical Rites" by Pauline Campanelli
- "Witchcraft and Healing" by Morwyn
- "Sex Magic" by Valerie Voigt
- "Men and Women in Witchcraft" by Janet and Stewart Farrar
- "Witches and the Earth" by Chas S. Clifton
- "The Solo Witch" by Heather O'Dell
- "Witchcraft and the Law" by Pete Pathfinder Davis
- "Witchcraft and Shamanism" by Grey Cat
- "Being a Pagan in a 9-to-5 World" by Valerie Voigt

Also included are additional resources for Wiccans including publications, mail order suppliers, Pagan organizations, computer bulletin boards and spe-cial-interest resources. The Principles of Wiccan Belief are also restated here.

0-87542-377-9, 208 pp., 5¼ x 8, softcover $9.95

Prices subject to change without notice.

WITCHCRAFT TODAY, BOOK TWO
Rites of Passage
edited by Chas S. Clifton

This book is about the ritual glue that binds Pagan culture. In contrast, much writing on modern Paganism, whether it be Witchcraft or some other form, seems to assume that the reader is a young, single adult—a "seeker." At most, the reader is seen as a member of a coven in their group made up of adults. This collection of writings, however, takes a wider view with the long-term goal of presenting a living Pagan culture. If modern Pagan traditions are to persist and have any effect on the world community in an overt way, they must encompass people of all ages, not just young adults. *Witchcraft Today, Book Two: Rites of Passage*, therefore, is organized according to some of life's significant markers: birth, puberty, adulthood, partnership, parenthood, Wicca conversion, maturity or eldership, and finally death. None of these occur in a social vacuum, but always in relation to other people.

- "Childbirth and Wiccaning," Patricia Telesco
- "Raising a Pagan Child," Karen Charboneau-Harrison
- "Between the Worlds: Late Adolescence and Early Adulthood in Modern Paganism," Anodea Judith
- "Working with the Underaged Seeker," Judy Harrow
- "Reflections on Conversion to Wicca," by Darcie
- "Initiation by Ordeal: Military Service as a Passage into Adulthood," by Judy Harrow
- "Handfasting: Marriage and the Modern Pagan," by Jeff Charboneau-Harrison
- "Puberty Rites for Adult Women," by Oz
- "Pagan Approaches to Illness, Grief and Loss," by Paul Suliin
- "Witches after 40," by Grey Cat
- "Pagan Rites of Dying," by Oz

0-87542-378-7, 288 pp., 5¼ x 8, softcover $9.95

Prices subject to change without notice.

WITCHCRAFT TODAY, BOOK THREE
Witchcraft & Shamanism
edited by Chas S. Clifton

This book is a compelling and honest examination of shamanic techniques (both classical and neo-) as they are being practiced in Neopagan Witchcraft in the 1990s. Shamanism is a natural adjunct to the ritualistic and magical practice of many covens and solitary Pagans. In this ground-breaking volume, you will discover how others have integrated techniques such as trance journeys, soul retrieval, and altered states of consciousness.

Discover how shamanic ideas influenced Greek philosophers, Platonists, Pythagoreans and Gnostics ... learn how evidence from the old witch trials suggests that at least some Europeans may have practiced shamanic journeying in the past ... incorporate caves for ritual and inner journeys, both literally and in visualization ... find out who is out there retrieving souls and curing elfshot ... compare the guided visualizations common to modern magickal practice with the neo-shamanic journey ... learn how spirit contacts are made, how guides are perceived and what "worlds" they reside in ... and much more.

1-56718-150-3, 288 pp., 5¼ x 8, photos, softcover $9.95

WICCA
A Guide for the Solitary Practitioner
Scott Cunningham

Wicca is a book of life, and how to live magically, spiritually, and wholly attuned with Nature. It is a book of sense and common sense, not only about Magick, but about religion and one of the most critical issues of today: how to achieve the much needed and wholesome relationship with our Earth. Cunningham presents Wicca as it is today: a gentle, Earth-oriented religion dedicated to the Goddess and God. This book fulfills a need for a practical guide to solitary Wicca—a need which no previous book has fulfilled.

Here is a positive, practical introduction to the religion of Wicca, designed so that any interested person can learn to practice the religion alone, any-where in the world. It presents Wicca honestly and clearly, without the pseudo-history that permeates other books. It shows that Wicca is a vital, satisfying part of twentieth century life.

This book presents the theory and practice of Wicca from an individual's perspective. The section on the Standing Stones Book of Shadows contains solitary rituals for the Esbats and Sabbats. This book, based on the author's nearly two decades of Wiccan practice, presents an eclectic picture of vari-ous aspects of this religion. Exercises designed to develop magical profi-ciency, a self-dedication ritual, herb, crystal and rune magic, recipes for Sabbat feasts, are included in this excellent book.

0-87542-118-0, 240 pp., 6 x 9, illus., softcover $9.95

Prices subject to change without notice.

BUCKLAND'S COMPLETE BOOK OF WITCHCRAFT
Raymond Buckland

Here is the most complete resource to the study and practice of modern, non-denominational Wicca. This is a lavishly illustrated, self-study course for the solitary or group. Included are rituals; exercises for developing psychic talents; information on all major "sects" of the Craft; sections on tools, beliefs, dreams, meditations, divination, herbal lore, healing, ritual clothing and much, much more. This book unites theory and practice into a comprehensive course designed to help you develop into a practicing Witch, one of the "Wise Ones." It is written by Ray Buckland, a very famous and respected authority on Witchcraft who first came public with the Old Religion in the United States. Large format with workbook-type exercises, profusely illustrated and full of music and chants. Takes you from A to Z in the study of Witchcraft.

Never before has so much information on the Craft of the Wise been collected in one place. Traditionally, there are three degrees of advancement in most Wiccan traditions. When you have completed studying this book, you will be the equivalent of a Third-Degree Witch. Even those who have practiced Wicca for years find useful information in this book, and many covens are using this for their textbook. If you want to become a Witch, or if you merely want to find out what Witchcraft is really about, you will find no better book than this.

0-87542-050-8, 272 pp., 8½ x 11, illus., softcover $14.95

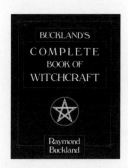

Prices subject to change without notice.